What would it mean to win?

turbulence collective

PM PRESS

ISBN: 978-1-60486-110-5
LCCN: 20100601

Turbulence are: David Harvie, Keir Milburn, Tadzio Mueller, Rodrigo Nunes,
Michal Osterweil, Kay Summer, Ben Trott, David Watts

This edition published by PM Press, 2010.

PM Press
PO Box 23912
Oakland, CA 94623
www.pmpress.org

Layout and cover art by briandesign
Printed in the USA, on recycled paper

Contents

Preface

Turbulence: What would it mean to win? was intended as a political intervention into the mobilisation against the 2007 G8 summit, held in Heiligendamm, on Germany's Baltic coast. It took the form of a 32-page newspaper and we printed 7,000 copies.

Response to *Turbulence* exceeded all our expectations. Bundles left at the various convergence centres and camps quickly shrank, disappeared and had to be replenished. We saw copies being read and discussed everywhere. Following the summit, we received requests for copies from individuals and groups around the world. People have translated articles in several other languages. The 14 texts we assembled clearly resonated within the movement. We soon ran out of copies.

Although all the articles are available on our website (www.turbulence.org.uk), we're delighted to see the whole back in print. This edition contains some addi-. tional material too. In the autumn 2007, we authored a piece entitled *Move into the Light? Postscript to a turbulent 2007*. This was published as a pamphlet in English and German and, as an article, in *Le Monde diplomatique Brasil*. We have included the text of *Move into the Light?* here. The book opens with a Foreword by John Holloway. It concludes with an extensive interview with two members of the collective, conducted in the winter and spring of 2008–2009.

Movements move. The original newspaper was conceived as a political intervention in the summer of 2007. Since then the problematics we face have shifted. There is a risk that some of the pieces may not seem as relevant as when they were written, but as a whole we feel they stand the test of time. The contributions were, after all, drawn from movements in different parts of the world, operating in different situations and at different stages in their cycle of struggles. Our question crossed such differences and remained relevant. Can't such a question also cross the gap between 2007 and now? Isn't it always both timely and untimely to ask the question "What would it mean to win?"

Turbulence Collective

David Harvie, Keir Milburn, Tadzio Mueller, Rodrigo Nunes, Michal Osterweil, Kay Summer, Ben Trott, David Watts
Berlin, Chapel Hill, Leeds, São Paulo
January 2010

Hope moves faster than the speed of thought

Foreword by John Holloway

I SHOULDN'T be here doing this, and yet I can't resist it, the honour of it. *Turbulence* is exciting. It's the restlessness of it, the itchiness of it, the refusal to rest on laurels, to be satisfied, the constant rethinking, re-posing of the problems, the going beyond itself, the moving beyond movements, the overflowing. A moving that disrupts, a turbulence. Not a cistern, but a fountain out of control.

Of course we should not be satisfied. How could we be when we still live in capitalism, when we still create and re-create capitalism each day, when we are all complicit in the production of a world that kills and humiliates and destroys? How can we live with that? And yet we do. We cannot be satisfied, and yet perhaps we are. As we scream and hurl ourselves against capital, we glance at our image in the mirror and fall in love with it. How romantic we are, how brave, how clever. We are blinded by what we see, captivated by it. "However hazy our image in the mirror has always been, have we not become too enamoured of it…?". We come to ourselves and something has happened. The movement has stopped. Or perhaps it is just our movement that has stopped, just we who have stopped. We are left there stranded, in danger of becoming one of "those strange political groups of yesteryear, arguing about 1917 or 1936, or whatever as worlds pass by". 1917 or 1936 or 1968 or 1994 or 2001 or 2008, perhaps. The danger is there all the time: we invent a word, the "Left", to pretend that we haven't been stranded, to hide our distancing from the flow of struggle, as a nostalgic memory of what we did in our youth, as a self-deception.

Turbulence does not let us do that: the word "Left" is hardly mentioned, there is no time for sitting back and nostalging. We must try and see what is wrong, how we can start moving again. If the movement of movements has run into difficulties, then we must try to get it moving again, nudge it in a new direction. "To recognise the limits of a particular moment or phase of struggle does not have to imply an inability to move beyond it." Just the contrary: we must do everything we can to find a way forward.

This cannot be done by laying down a new line. Even if we wanted to, there is no one who could do it. The articles in this collection are contributions to a discussion. They share a common concern, but not a common solution. They are all prompted by the question of "What would it mean to win?", but one feels that there is really another question that motivates them all: how do we get going again? Or perhaps, what is to be done now? They are all very honest reflections (and though I do not mention all by name, I found them each and all very stimulating). Gone, thank goodness, are the revolutionary recipes of the past, the answers.

There is no common line, but there are themes that recur in several of the articles. Three of them strike me as being particularly important.

The first is demands. Do we think of nudging the movement forward in terms of the reformulation of demands? Ben Trott, basing himself on current discussions in Germany, suggests that the formulation of directional demands may be a way forward. Yet, however much the directional demands may differ from transitional or other demands, there is, as the Free Association point out, always a problem with demands: they are always addressed to somebody, they always carry with them the tonality of asking somebody for something. The notion of a demand already suggests the acceptance that power is external to us. Power is indeed outside us, but our struggle is to dissolve the externality of power, to re-appropriate the world as ours. Or better: our struggle is to stop externalising our power, to stop alienating the world from ourselves. The danger with demands, however directional, is that we are not just recognising an external power but actually creating that power, converting our power-to into an external power-over. Gustavo Esteva suggests that in effect we should forget about demanding anything and just get on with creating the world we want. Forget about changing the world and get on with constructing a new one (or new ones). Live the world we want to create: that stands as the alternative to a politics of demands. We assume our own power to create, and refuse to project it on to anyone else and recognise it as their power over us.

Of course it is not so simple. The Free Association, who prefer to think of problematics rather than demands (for the reasons already mentioned), nevertheless point out that the formulation of demands can give coherence to a movement, give it an identity. With this, we are back with the problem of the image in the mirror. To have an identity is to look in the mirror and see our image. Harmless enough perhaps, or perhaps necessary though harmful. This is the issue of institutionalisation. We were clear that the Communist Party, that great Revolutionary Institution, was a major obstacle to the flow of anti-capitalist struggle. And then we saw that all revolutionary parties are obstacles to the moving of struggle, and we thought that with that we had got rid of the problem of institutionalisation. But now we see that our image in the mirror is a new form of institutionalisation that blinds us just as surely (though perhaps less crudely) to the moving of the movement. The *Turbulence* group concludes in *Move into the Light?* that "Perhaps the impasse of the last few years has arisen precisely because people have failed to see answers in the places they searched, and did not start looking elsewhere. However hazy our image in the mirror has always been, have we not become too enamoured of it to actually have a look around?" Institutions, however anti-institutional, make us insensitive, stop us listening to the responses to the questions we walk asking, make us blind to the moving of struggle. Institutions, however anti-institutional, seek to freeze the flow of time. But do we not need them? Sandro Mezzadro and Gigi Roggero suggest that we should seek a new institutionality, but I feel that this is to move in the wrong direction: taking the world into our own hands, assuming our own power-to, means that we try to swim (or skate or fly) without holding on to the edge for security. Perhaps we cannot live with such intensity, perhaps we need to rest from our moments of excess, but then at best we should think of institutions as a resting stage, a place to sit down and consider how to move on – which is precisely what *Turbulence* is about.

Only we should not think that if we stop for a moment, the world will necessarily stop with us. The struggle flows on. Beyond the movements that produce images in the mirror, there is an "endless moving of social relations" that seems to leave no visible trace. Hope moves faster than either perception or thought. The *Turbulence* group cite the struggles in the *banlieues* of France as a moving of struggle beyond the movement in struggle, and Euclides Andrés Mance points to a much less dramatic moving when he says: "there is a global revolution underway. It is not led by any political party or vanguard. It has no military bases and its strategy is anti-belligerent. It mobilises millions of people all over the world. We know little about it." With this he refers to the "solidarity economics", a term that I don't like because of its ambiguities and its reproduction of the idea of the economic as a distinct sphere of life-activity, but which nevertheless points to the millions and millions of people who are simply trying, by choice or necessity, to break out of the logic of capitalist labour, and who probably do not go to the anti-G8 summits and may not even have heard of them. Heiligendamm and the other anti-summits are at most the tip of an iceberg, the most visible manifestations of a much deeper, darker, broader moving against-and-beyond capital. To resolve the stutter in the flow of the movement of movements, perhaps we need to focus on the relation between the movement and this deeper moving. This book is an important opening in this direction.

And it's fun.

turbulence
ideas for movement

WHO WE ARE

Welcome to the first issue of *Turbulence*, a journal-cum-newspaper that we hope will become an ongoing space in which to think through, debate and articulate the political, social, economic and cultural theories of our movements, as well as the networks of diverse practices and alternatives that surround them.

This issue is the first stage in a collective project, and we hope it will be a worthwhile contribution to ongoing discussions, debates and processes of reflection within the global 'movement of movements' and beyond. As with any such project, however, it has its shortcomings. Important issues and struggles are not covered (for example, there's nothing about last year's massive struggles against the 'First Employment Law' (CPE) in France nor anything about the first World Social Forum held in Africa), there's a bias towards the global North (in terms of both the location/origin of contributors and perspective) and women's voices are largely absent. Whilst we believe that it is not possible to 'represent' a movement, especially one as complex as ours – movements can only be sampled, and the position we do this from always influences the result – we nevertheless recognise these shortcomings as genuine problems for which we also share responsibility.

We don't want *Turbulence* to become yet another journal or yet another edited collection claiming to offer a 'snapshot of the movement'. Instead we want to carve out a space where we can carry out difficult debates and investigations into the political realities of our time – engaging the real differences in vision, analysis and strategy that exist among our movements.

David Harvie, Keir Milburn, Tadzio Mueller, Rodrigo Nunes, Michal Osterweil,
Kay Summer, Ben Trott, David Watts
May 2007

January 2010 update

The first issue of *Turbulence: Ideas for Movement* was published in June 2007 and we published the Postscript (also included in this edition) in December of the same year. Since then, we have produced two full-length issues, *Who will save us from the future?* (July 2008) and *And now for something completely different?* (December 2009). We still have a few copies of both these later issues available and both can be read online at www.turbulence.org.uk.

Are we "winning"?

Turbulence Collective

'WE ARE WINNING' This slogan, spray-painted on a wall, was one of the most iconic images of the protests against the Third Ministerial meeting of the World Trade Organisation (WTO) in Seattle in 1999. It captured the sentiment of the moment on that crazy rainy winter morning perfectly. Seemingly out of nowhere, a decade after the supposed 'end of history', a coalition of anarchists and communists, environmentalists and trade unionists, nuns and queers, and thousands of others had taken to the streets, and actually shut down the WTO conference in Microsoft's and Starbucks' home town. How did that happen?

Many describe Seattle as our movement's 'coming-out party'. For we didn't emerge out of nowhere; a multitude of struggles had been slowly growing in the shadows... Against World Bank mega-projects, like the Narmada dam in India. Against the privatisation of public utilities, such as water struggles in South Africa. Against the enclosure of land with movements in Brazil and the Zapatistas in Mexico. Against employment reforms, like the ship-building and automobile strikes in South Korea. And against the meeting of the G7 heads of state, like the global day of action on June 18, 1999, the last time they met in Germany. The movement didn't begin in Seattle, but its importance lay in its resonance both in the city's streets and well beyond. It was a moment of intensity – none of us were alone anymore – even if we'd never been to Seattle or seen a WTO representative.

In the years which followed, lines of resistance and creation – the production of other worlds – could be traced around the world. These were lines which connected the counter-summit mobilisations in Washington DC, Chiang Mai, Prague, Quebec and Genoa. They linked European social centres with farmers' struggles in India; the Argentinian *piqueteros* with free software movements; struggles for free access to education and knowledge with those against biotechnology. Spaces – both real and virtual – were created to build, strengthen and develop networks of resistance and creation: Peoples' Global Action, the Indymedia news network, the World Social Forum and hundreds of local versions. We were caught up in a new cycle of struggles; there was a real 'affect of winning'. This wasn't just a feeling, experienced by us as individuals or in groups. It was an increase in our power of acting, which allowed us as a movement to engage in new modes of behaviour.

WAR

Some say that the last time they saw the 'We Are Winning' slogan, it was sprayed on the side of a burning police van in Genoa, as the G8 met in the summer of 2001. Has it seemed appropriate since? Today winning seems a long way off.

Some see Genoa as a turning point. It marked the end of a cycle of struggles and the beginning of a new one – an attempt to instigate a global, open-ended police-war. This war was declared with a series of violent attacks upon both the flesh and bones of those considered somehow 'militant', but also much more indiscriminately, against the whole of the social body seen as constituting this other possible world. This war was of course not new, in history or in the present; but it would become generalised and intensified following the events of September 11, a few months later. More than

WHY HEILIGENDAMM?

We published *Turbulence* to coincide with the counter-mobilisation against the G8 summit in Heiligendamm, Germany in June 2007. There were three reasons for this. First, we saw *Turbulence* as a political intervention. Summit mobilisations have played a significant part in this recent eruption of struggle, but many of us were asking how we could move beyond them. Second, we had found counter-summit mobilisations to be moments of extraordinary collective openness: different ideas of how to change the world often make more sense in these moments than they do in the rest of our lives. Third, while we planned to make *Turbulence* available around the world, in multiple formats (print, audio download, on-line translations), in Heiligendamm we hoped to reach thousands of people who might not otherwise pick up a copy in the usual radical infoshops, or surf past our website.

a matter of localised moments of repression, war has again clearly become one of the ways in which the world is run: not 'the continuation of politics through other means', but a means by which life is managed. The affects of winning – bound up with the joyful experience of desire creating another world – are replaced by those of fear, and the apparent omnipresence of a power turned against us. And what next?

WHAT WOULD IT MEAN TO WIN?

Movements become apparent as 'movements' at times of acceleration and expansion. In these heady moments they have fuzzy boundaries, no membership lists – everybody is too engaged in what's coming next, in creating the new, looking to the horizon. But movements get blocked, they slow down, they cease to move, or continue to move without considering their actual effects. When this happens, they can stifle new developments, suppress the emergence of new forms of politics; or fail to see other possible directions. Many movements just stop functioning as movements. They become those strange political groups of yesteryear, arguing about 1917 or 1936, or whatever as worlds pass by.

Sometimes all it takes to get moving again is a nudge in a new direction. Take the example of the *Movimento Sem Terra*, Brazil's landless peasants movement: in the 1980s they were successfully getting land, more and more, but they ceased to actually move. They merely repeated a cycle. Many got land, but almost all lost it too: the landless-to-farmer transition was too much too fast. They got eaten and spat out by land speculators and banks. Then the movement changed direction. They put their energy into keeping people on the land, not getting more, and later used those secure bases to intensify their struggle for more land. Result: one million families have settled themselves on what was once big ranchers' land.

UNCOMFORTABLE WITH WINNING?

Some people are uncomfortable with the notion of winning. This is because winning implies that some will be losers. Of course in healthy relationships winning and losing can be seriously damaging. If conversations are approached with the aim of 'winning', then the conversation will, at best, not be productive. In most relationships winning and losing should have no place. The relationship, what you're doing in the relationship, is more important. But does this extend to situations of domination, such as the daily conversation we have with capitalism? What if somebody is physically attacking you? Isn't winning – whether through escape or defeat – in those situations more important than the relationship? Isn't it in fact the relationship that ought to be destroyed or made irrelevant? Winning need not imply a zero-sum game, but at times it might be a matter of life and death. In such situations it seems essential to do more than just pose the question of how to be effective. To think of winning. To try. Hard.
(Based on a section in Derrick Jensen's *Endgame, Volume II: Resistance*)

We also want more movement, new directions. Who doesn't? So we think now is a good time to ask the question: **What would – or could – it mean to 'win'?**

The question is important because it opens up so many others. It may nudge us in new directions. Take just three:

- **How do we understand contemporary capitalism, and what would it mean to break with it?**
- **How do we deal with living on a finite planet, and with its manifestations such as climate change?**
- **How different is the global movement of movements from all that has passed before; and how can we learn from history?**

Strangely these all lead to somewhat similar questions: politically, why do we do what we do, and why do we keep doing it? And of course: what (else) could be done?

We're not offering a packaged and polished set of answers to these or any other questions. The 14 articles in *Turbulence* come from different contexts, different parts of the world; they have different tones, different paces and they certainly don't all agree with each other; and some are harder than others to read outside their context. But we think this unevenness, what some might call roughness, is useful. It's sometimes hard to engage with a collection of texts which is too polished. You've no sooner exclaimed, 'that's wrong, I don't agree with that at all!' or 'but what about X?', than the author's anticipated your objection in a footnote, or else the editors have directed you to another article which plugs the gap. On the other hand, rough edges provide handholds, something to grab onto. They provide a way into arguments. Maybe you'll pull at a loose end and everything will unravel. But perhaps you'll be able to

WHY 'TURBULENCE'?

Turbulence is the disruption caused by movement through a non-moving element or an element moving at a different speed, which seems somehow apt for this project.

Consider the flow of water over a simple smooth object, such as a sphere. At very low speeds the flow is laminar, ie the flow is smooth (though it may involve vortices on a large scale). As the speed increases, at some point the transition is made to turbulent ('chaotic') flow. You can see the same thing when you turn on a tap.

But although the complete description of turbulence remains one of the unsolved problems in physics, this chaotic flow is enormously productive. Insects fly in a sea of vortices, surrounded by tiny eddies and whirlwinds that are created when they move their wings. For years, scientists said that, theoretically, the bumblebee should not be able to fly, as its wings are so small relative to its body's mass: an airplane built with the same proportions would never get off the ground. For conventional aerodynamics, turbulence is a problem to be controlled and eliminated. But once we take turbulence into account as a productive force, then it's easy to see how bumblebee wings produce more lift than predicted by conventional aerodynamic analyses. The aerodynamics are incredibly unsteady and difficult to analyse, but it works!

weave something else with those threads. What we want to do is put out articles that help us to think new thoughts. To think and act *differently*.

But there is a common thread running through the articles: it's that we think the questions they tackle are essential if we are to have any chance of turning the world upside down. Are we alone in this? We don't think so. Recently we've come across different initiatives where we've glimpsed the outlines of new re-groupings. We're not proclaiming 'the time is now'. Nor are we demanding 'one more push, comrades'. It's more subtle than that. More tentative. Will we be swept up again? Maybe. Will a high tide come from an unexpected direction? Probably. And what's *Turbulence* got to do with it? Who knows? But you can't say you haven't been warned that people are experimenting. And some of those experiments will get out of control.

Politics in an age of fantasy

Stephen Duncombe

REALITY, FANTASY AND POLITICS

In the autumn of 2004, shortly before the U.S. presidential election and in the middle of a typically bloody month in Iraq, *The New York Times Magazine* ran a feature article on the casualty of truth in the Bush administration. Like most *Times* articles, it was well written, well researched, and thoroughly predictable. That George W. Bush is ill-informed, doesn't listen to dissenting opinion, and acts upon whatever nonsense he happens to believe is hardly news. (Even the fact that he once insisted that Sweden did not have an army and none of his cabinet dared contradict him was not all that surprising.) There was, however, one valuable insight. In a soon-to-be-infamous passage, the writer, Ron Suskind, recounted a conversation between himself and an unnamed senior adviser to the president:

> The aide said that guys like me were "in what we call the reality-based community," which he defined as people who "believe that solutions emerge from your judicious study of discernable reality." I nodded and murmured something about Enlightenment principles and empiricism. He cut me off. "That's not the way the world really works anymore," he continued. "We're an empire now, and when we act, we create reality. And while you are studying that reality – judiciously, as you will – we'll act again creating other new realities, which you can study too, and that's how things will sort out. We're history's actors … and you, all of you, will be left to just study what we do."

It was clear how the *Times* felt about this peek into the political mind of the presidency. The editors of the Grey Lady pulled out the passage and floated it over the article in oversized, multi-colored type. This was ideological gold: the Bush administration openly and arrogantly admitting that they didn't care about reality. One could almost feel the palpable excitement generated among the *Times'* liberal readership, an enthusiasm mirrored and amplified all down the left side of the political spectrum on computer listservs, call-in radio shows, and print editorials over the next few weeks. This proud assertion of naked disregard for reality and unbounded faith in fantasy was the most damning evidence of Bush insanity yet. He must surely lose the election now.

What worried me then, and still worries me today, is that my reaction was radically different. My politics have long been diametrically opposed to those of the Bush administration, and I've had a long career as a left-leaning academic and a progressive political activist. Yet I read the same words that generated so much animosity among liberals and the Left and felt something else: excited, inspired – and jealous. Whereas the commonsense view held that Bush's candid disregard for reality was evidence of the madness of his administration, I perceived it as a much more disturbing sign of its brilliance. I knew then that Bush, in spite of making a mess of nearly everything he had undertaken in his first presidential term, would be reelected.

How could my reaction be so different from that of so many of my colleagues and comrades? Maybe I was becoming a neocon, another addition to the long list of defectors whose progressive God had failed. Would I follow the path of Christopher Hitchens? A truly depressing thought. But what if, just maybe, the problem was not with me but with the main currents of progressive thinking in this country? More precisely, maybe there was something about progressive politics that had become increasingly problematic. The problem, as I see it, comes down to reality. Progressives believe in it, Bush's people believe in creating it. The Left and Right have switched roles – the right taking on the mantle of radicalism and progressives waving the flag of conservatism. The political progeny of the protestors who proclaimed, "Take your desires for reality" in May of 1968, were now counseling the reversal: take reality for your desires. Republicans were the ones proclaiming, "I have a dream."

Progressive dreams, and the spectacles that give them tangible form, will look different than those conjured up by the Bush administration or the commercial directors of what critic Neil Gabler calls *life: the movie*. Different not only in content – this should be obvious – but in form. Given the progressive ideals of egalitarianism and a politics that values the input of everyone, our dreamscapes will not be created by media-savvy experts of the Left and then handed down to the rest of us to watch, consume, and believe. Instead, our spectacles will be participatory: dreams the public can mold and shape themselves. They will be active: spectacles that work only if people help create them. They will be open-ended: setting stages to ask questions and leaving silences to formulate answers. And they will be transparent: dreams that one knows are dreams but which still have power to attract and inspire. And, finally, the spectacles we create will not cover over or replace reality and truth but perform and amplify it. Illusion may be a necessary part of political life, but delusion need not be.

Perhaps the most important reason for progressives to make their peace with the politics of dreaming has little to do with the immediate task of winning consent or creating dissent, but has instead to do with long-term vision. Without dreams we will never be able to imagine the new world we want to build. From the 1930s until the 1980s political conservatives in this country were lost: out of power and out of touch. Recalling those days, Karl Rove, George W. Bush's senior political adviser, says: "We were relegated to the desert." While many a pragmatic Republican moved to the center, a critical core kept wandering in that desert, hallucinating a political world considered fantastic by postwar standards: a preemptive military, radical tax cuts, eroding the line between church and state, ending welfare, and privatizing Social Security. Look where their dreams are today.

PARTICIPATORY SPECTACLE

All spectacle counts on popular participation. The fascist rallies in Japan, Italy, and Germany; the military parades through Moscow's Red Square; the halftime shows at the Super Bowl – all demand an audience to march, stand, or do the wave. Even the more individualistic spectacle of advertising depends upon the distant participation of the spectator, who must become a consumer. But the public in both fascist and commercial spectacles only participates from the outside, as a set piece on a stage imagined and directed by someone else. As Siegfried Kracauer, a German film critic writing in the 1920s about "the mass ornament," the public spectacles that prefigured Nazi rallies, observed, "Although the masses give rise to the ornament, they are not involved in thinking it through."

Ethical spectacle demands a different sort of participation. The people who participate in the performance of the spectacle must also contribute to its construction. As opposed to the spectacles of commercialism and fascism, the public in an ethical spectacle is not considered a stage prop, but a co-producer and co-director. This is nothing radical, merely the application of democratic principles to the spectacles that govern our lives. If it is reasonable to demand that we have a say in how our schools are run or who is elected president, why shouldn't we have the right to participate in the planning and carrying out of spectacle?

A participatory spectacle is not a spontaneous one; an organizer... needs to set the stage for participation to happen. But the mission of the organizer of an ethical spectacle differs from that of other spectacles. She has her eyes on two things. First is the overall look of the spectacle – that is, the desires being expressed, the dreams being displayed, the outcome being hoped for. In this way her job is the same as the fascist propagandist or the Madison Avenue creative director. But then she has another job. She must create a situation in which popular participation not only *can* happen but *must* happen for the spectacle to come to fruition.

The theorist/activists of the Situationists made a useful distinction between spectacle and situation. The spectacle they condemned as a site of "nonintervention"; there was simply no space for a spectator to intervene in what he or she was watching because it demanded only passivity and acquiescence. The Situationists saw it as their mission to fight against "the society of the spectacle," but they also felt a responsibility to set something else in motion to replace it. "We must try and construct situations," their master theorist Guy Debord wrote in 1957. These "situations" were no less staged events than fascist rallies, but their goal was different. The Situationists encouraged people to *dérive* – drift through unfamiliar city streets – and they showed mass culture films after "detourning" the dialogue, dubbing the actor's lines to comment upon (or make nonsense of) the film being shown and the commercial culture from which it came. These situations, it was hoped, would create "collective ambiances," which encouraged participants to break out of the soporific routine of the society of the spectacle and participate in the situation unfolding around them: to make sense of new streets and sights, look at celluloid images in a new and different way, and thereby alter people's relationship to their material and media environment. As Debord wrote: "The role played by a passive or merely bit-playing 'public' must constantly diminish, while that played by those who cannot be called actors but rather, in a new sense of the term, 'livers,' must steadily increase." Whereas actors play out a tight script written by another, "livers" write their own script through their actions within a given setting. The ideal of the "situation" was to set the stage for "transformative action."

TRANSPARENT SPECTACLE

Spectacle needn't pass itself off as reality to be effective in engaging the spectator. At least this was the hope of the playwright Bertolt Brecht. Brecht was disturbed by what he saw of the theater that surrounded him in Germany between the wars. With most theater (and movies and TV) the goal is to construct an illusion so complete that the audience will be drawn away from their world and into the fantasy on stage. This seduction is essential to traditional dramaturgy. First theorized by Aristotle in his *Poetics*, it stresses audience identification with the drama on stage: when an actor cries, you are supposed to cry; when he triumphs, you triumph as well. This allure is aided by staging that strives toward realism or captivates the audience with lavish displays of full-blown fantasy... Such drama "works" insofar as the audience is well entertained, but there is a political cost. Entranced, the audience suspends critical thought, and all action is sequestered to the stage. A "cowed, credulous, hypnotized mass," Brecht described these spectators, "these people seem relieved of activity and like men to whom something is being done. It's a pretty accurate description of the problem with most spectacle.

As a progressive, Brecht was horrified by this response of the theatergoing audience. He wanted to use his plays to motivate people to change the world, not escape from it. He understood that no matter how radical the content of his plays might be, if his audience lost itself in the illusion of his play and allowed the actors to do the action for them, then they would leave their politics up on the stage when the play was over.

Brecht believed that one could change the way drama is done and thus change its impact on the audience. Borrowing from the Chinese stage, he developed a dramaturgical method called epic theater. Central to epic theater was the *Verfremdungseffekt*, a term he mercilessly shortened to the V-effect, which, translated into English, means roughly "alienation effect." Instead of drawing people into a seamless illusion, Brecht strove to push them away – to alienate them – so that they would never forget that they were watching a play.

To accomplish the V-effect, Brecht and others, notably the Berlin director Erwin Piscator, who staged many of Brecht's plays, developed a whole battery of innovative techniques: giving away the ending of the play at the beginning, having actors remind the audience that they are actors, humorous songs which interrupt tragic scenes, music which runs counter to mood, cue cards informing the audience that a scene is changing, stagehands appearing on stage to move props, and so on. Brecht even championed the idea of a "smokers' theater" with the stage shrouded in thick smoke exhaled by a cigar-puffing audience – anything to break the seamless illusion of traditional theater.

While the function of the V-effect was to alienate his audience, it is a misreading of Brecht's intentions to think that he wanted to create a theater that couldn't be enjoyed. Nothing could be further from his mind. He heaped ridicule on an avant garde that equated unpopularity with artistic integrity and insisted that the job of the dramaturge is to entertain, demanding that theater be "enjoyable to the senses." For both political and dramaturgical reasons he rejected the preaching model of persuasion; he wanted his audiences to have fun, not attend a lecture. Deconstructing the mind/body binary, Brecht believed that one could speak to reason and the senses. One could see through the spectacle and enjoy it nonetheless: a transparent spectacle.

Brecht's V-effect has been adopted, in some cases quite consciously, by some of the more theatrical activist groups. Recall the Billionaires for Bush. Wearing long gowns and tiaras, tuxedos and top hats, the activists playing billionaires don't hope to pass themselves off as the real thing. Real billionaires wear artfully distressed designer jeans; these Billionaires look like characters out of a game of *Monopoly*. Because their artifice is obvious, there is no deception of their audience. They are not seen as people who *are*, but instead as people who *are presenting*. Because of this the Billionaires' message of wealth inequality and the corruption of money on politics is not passively absorbed by spectators identifying with character or scene, but consciously understood by an audience watching an obvious performance.

Furthermore, the spectacle the Billionaires present is so patently playacted, so unnatural, that the absurd unnaturality of a caucus of "people of wealth" advocating for their own rights is highlighted. This is, of course, what American democracy has become: a system where money buys power to protect money. This is no secret, but that's part of the problem. The corruption of democracy is so well known that it is tacitly accepted as the natural course of things. One of the functions of the V-effect is to alienate the familiar: to take what is common sense and ask why it is so common – as Brecht put it: "to free socially conditioned phenomena from that stamp of familiarity which protects them against our grasp today." By acting out the roles of obviously phony billionaires buying politicians for their own advantage, the Billionaires encourage the viewer of their spectacle to step back and look critically at the taken-for-grantedness of a political system where money has a voice, prodding them to question: "Isn't it really the current political system that's absurd?" The transparency of the spectacle allows the spectator to look through what is being presented to the reality of what is there.

Unlike the opaque spectacles of commercialism and fascism, which always make claims to the truth, a progressive spectacle invites the viewer to see through it: to acknowledge its essential "falsity" while being moved by it nonetheless. Most spectacle strives for seamlessness; ethical spectacle reveals its own workings. Most spectacle employs illusion in the pretense of portraying reality; ethical spectacle demonstrates the reality of its own illusions. Ethical spectacle reminds the viewer that the spectacle is never reality, but always a spectacle. In this way, ironically, spectacle becomes real.

REAL SPECTACLE

For spectacle to be ethical it must not only reveal itself as what it is but also have as its foundation something real. At this point it is worth reiterating my initial argument that to embrace spectacle does not mean a radical rejection of the empirical real and the verifiably true. It is merely acknowledging that the real and the true are not self-evident: they need to be told and sold. The goal of the ethical spectacle is not to replace the real with the spectacle, but to reveal and amplify the real *through* the spectacle. Think of this as an inversion of Secretary of State Colin Powell's infamous case to the United Nations for war in Iraq. Armed with reasoned reports and documentary photos of Saddam Hussein's nuclear ambitions, Powell employed the tools of fact to make the case for the full-blown fantasy of Iraq's possession of weapons of mass destruction. Ethical spectacle employs the opposite strategy: the tools of spectacle as a way to mobilize support for the facts. As such, an ethical spectacle must start with reality.

An ethical spectacle must address the real dreams and desires of people – not the dreams and desires that progressives think they should, could, or "if they knew what was good for them" would have, but the ones people actually do have, no matter how trivial, politically incorrect, or even impossible they seem. How we address these dreams and desires is a political decision, but we must acknowledge and respond to them if we want people to identify with our politics. To engage the real as part of an ethical spectacle is not the same thing as being limited by the current confines of reality. For reality is not the end but a point of beginning – a firm foundation on which to build the possible, or to stand upon while dreaming the impossible.

21

DREAM SPECTACLE

The poet Eduardo Galeano writes of utopia:

> She's on the horizon… I go two steps, she moves two steps away. I walk ten steps and the horizon runs ten steps ahead. No matter how much I walk, I'll never reach her. What good is utopia? That's what: it's good for walking.

This is the goal of the ethical spectacle as well. The error is to see the spectacle as the new world. This is what both fascist and commercial spectacle does, and in this way the spectacle becomes a replacement for dreaming. Ethical spectacle offers up a different formulation. Instead of a dream's replacement, the ethical spectacle is a dream put on display. It is a dream that we can watch, think about, act within, try on for size, yet necessarily never realize. The ethical spectacle is a means, like the dreams it performs, to imagine new ends. As such, the ethical spectacle has the possibility of *creating* an outside – as an illusion. This is not the delusion of believing that you have created an outside, but an illusion that gives direction and motivation that might just get you there.

I would love to give an example of the ideal ethical spectacle, one which incorporates all the properties listed above. I can't. There isn't one. The ideal ethical spectacle is like a dream itself: something to work, and walk, toward. Progressives have a lot of walking to do. We need to do this with our feet on the ground, with a clear understanding of the real (and imaginary) terrain of the country. But we also need to dream, for without dreams we won't know where we are walking to.

Progressive dreams, to have any real political impact, need to become popular dreams. This will only happen if they resonate with the dreams that people already have – like those expressed in commercial culture today, and even those manifested through fascism in the past. But for progressive dreams to stand a chance of becoming popular, they, too, need to be displayed. Our dreams do little good locked inside our heads and sequestered within our small circles; they need to be heard and seen, articulated and performed – yelled from the mountaintop. This is the job of spectacle. Spectacle is already part of our political and economic life; the important question is whose ethics does it embody and whose dreams does it express.

© *2007 Stephen Duncombe*

Stephen Duncombe's new book *Dream: Re-imagining Progressive Politics in an Age of Fantasy* makes the case for a progressive politics that embraces fantasy and spectacle, images and symbols, emotion and desire. In essence, a new political aesthetic: a kind of dreampolitik, created not simply to further existing progressive agendas but to help us imagine new ones. These are extracts from the book, which was published by The New Press in January 2007. For more details about the book, the author and the publishers check out www.dreampolitik.org or www.thenewpress.com.

Enclosing the enclosers

Gustavo Esteva

FROM JUNE TO OCTOBER, 2006, no police were seen in the city of Oaxaca, Mexico, (600,000 inhabitants), not even traffic police. The governor and all of his officials were reduced to meeting secretly in hotels and private homes; none dared come to work. The Popular Assembly of the Peoples of Oaxaca (APPO) had continued sit-ins around the clock in front of Oaxaca City's public buildings, as well as in the private and public radio and television stations it had in its hands. One night, a convoy of 35 SUVs, with undercover agents and mercenaries, drove by the sit-ins and began shooting. They were not aiming at the people, but trying to intimidate them. APPO reported the situation instantaneously on its radio stations, and within minutes people organised barricades to stop the convoy. After that experience, every night at 11pm more than a thousand barricades closed the streets around the sit-ins and at critical crossroads, to be opened again at 6am to facilitate circulation. In spite of the guerrilla attacks by the police, a human rights organisation reported that in those months there was less violence in Oaxaca than in any other similar period in the last 10 years. Many services, like garbage collection, were operated by their corresponding unions, all also participants of APPO.

Were we winning? Some analysts started to talk about the Oaxaca Commune. Smiling, some Oaxacans commented: 'Yes, but the Paris Commune lasted only 50 days; we have been here for more than 100 days.' No matter how pertinent, this historical analogy is an exaggeration except for the logical reaction both initiatives provoked in the power structure. In the same style in which the European armies crushed the communards, Mexican Federal Police, with the support of the Army and the Navy, were finally sent to deal with the uprising.

When the Federal Police arrived, on October 28, APPO decided to resist non-violently, avoiding confrontation. In the face of the police, with all their aggressive equipment, the people of Oaxaca exhibited enormous restraint. Unarmed citizens stopped the tanks by laying their own bodies on the pavement. Adults held back young people trying to express their anger. When the police reached the main plaza, APPO abandoned it and regrouped on the campus of the university. The police began selectively capturing APPO members at the barricades or in their homes. By the end of the day, there were three dead, many injured, and many more disappeared. Those picked up by the police were sequestered in military barracks.

For months, the government and the media condemned APPO in the name of law, order, public security, human rights, and stable institutions. All these elements were employed to justify the use of police force. But without realising it, the authorities gave us a lesson in revolutionary civics. The Federal Police became the vehicle for a massive violation of human rights: searches and arrests were carried out without warrants while the number of dead, wounded and disappeared increased. Only vigilantes of the dominant party and the government's own hired guns were allowed to travel freely.

Many were afraid that we would not be able to stop the bloodbath the governor and federal government seemed determined to provoke. In spite of APPO's continual appeal to non-violence, the people of Oaxaca felt deeply offended and angry. Moreover they didn't want to be cowards... What could we do confronted by this barbaric, irrational violence of the state against its own people? How do we deal with the mounting anger of the youngsters, after months of constant vigilance on the barricades?

On November 2 the people resisted an attack on the University by the Federal Police. The clash was the largest between civilians and police in Mexico's history, and perhaps the only one that resulted in an unquestionable popular triumph. The fight was certainly unequal enough: although the police were outnumbered five or six to one if we count children, they had shields and other weapons, not to mention tanks and helicopters, while the people had only sticks, stones, rockets (fireworks), a few slingshots, and some uninvited molotov cocktails.

Following this victory, the largest march in the history of Oaxaca took place on November 5: almost a quarter of the 3.5 million Oaxacans came to it. Among the participants were scores of indigenous authorities from communities throughout the state who came to the capital carrying their staffs of office to publicly declare their allegiance to the movement. (Oaxaca is the only state in Mexico where two thirds of the population are indigenous).

In order to strengthen our coordinating bodies we had a 'constitutive congress'. The last session of the exhausting meeting ended at 5am on Monday, November 13. Some 1,500 state delegates attended this peculiar assembly. A Council of 260 delegates was created, in order to coordinate the collective effort. They were to 'represent' everyone; indigenous peoples, of course, but also every sector of society. Some barricades also sent delegates to the Congress and they now have a representation in the Council. The Congress approved a charter for APPO, an action plan, and a code of conduct. Most of the agreements were reached through consensus. Some of them were very difficult. It was not easy to agree on gender equity, for example, but we reached a good agreement: everyone recognised that women had been at the forefront, in all aspects of the struggle, and had given to it its meaning and soul. One of the easiest agreements was the decision to give the struggle a clearly anti-capitalist orientation.

During the Congress the city was still occupied by the police. Eight more people disappeared that night. But 'they cannot occupy our soul', said one member of the Council. 'We have more freedom than ever.'

ARE WE THUS WINNING?

On January 20, 2007, the International Civil Commission for Observation of Human Rights presented its preliminary report – after collecting hundreds of testimonies and documents, most of them focused on the massive, violent repression of November 25. The Commission reported 23 documented and identified dead and others disappeared but unidentified for lack of formal report. People are afraid. 'They disappeared one of my sons. If I report it, they will disappear the other,' said an old woman. Hundreds were injured and arbitrarily detained, and all kinds of abuses and violations of human rights – including torture and sexual abuses – were committed against them. For the Commission,

> What happened in Oaxaca was the linking of a juridical and military strategy with psychosocial and community components. Its final purpose is to achieve the control and intimidation of the civil population especially in areas in which processes of citizen organisation and non party social movements are developing.

Are we winning? Is it enough to win to learn as much as we learned, about ourselves, our strengths and autonomy, and about the system oppressing us?

SOME BACKGROUND

For almost two years, the people of Oaxaca were in increasing turmoil. The immediate cause was the corrupt and authoritarian administration of Governor Ulises Ruiz, who took office after a fraudulent election in December 2004. But as the Oaxaqueños resisted Ruiz, deeper struggles came to the surface and began to find expression in a process of awakening, organisation, and radicalisation.

On May 22, 2006, the teachers union, with 70,000 members throughout the state, began a sit-in in Oaxaca City's main plaza in order to dramatise their economic plight. They did not get much attention or solidarity from the public. But on June 14 the governor ordered a violent repression of the sit-in. This episode changed the nature of the mobilisation, unifying large numbers of Oaxacans with their own reasons for opposing Ruiz's misrule. Overnight ¡Fuera Ulises! ('Out with Ulises!')

became the popular slogan in Oaxaca's neighborhoods and streets. On June 20 hundreds of social and grassroots organisations invented APPO.

All this has happened within a profound political transition in which Mexico is currently engaged. Our ancient régime is dead. Economic and political elites are attempting to substitute it with a 'neoliberal republic', while the social majorities are trying to reorganise society from the bottom up to create a new regime.

Over the last 25 years corrupt leaders who control public institutions have almost succeeded in completely dismantling them. Some were driven by market fundamentalism, others by greed or ambition. While their acts often shock us, enrage us, and even lead some of us to experience a kind of paralysis, sometimes they serve to awaken autonomous action among the people.

As Marx wrote in a letter to Ruge, 'what we have to do is undertake a critique of everything that is established, and to criticise without mercy, fearing neither the conclusions we reach nor our clash with the existing powers.' This is all the more pertinent when those powers opt for violence in an attempt to solve conflicts they are incapable of resolving peacefully and democratically, as in the current impasse in Oaxaca. Their use of force can cause great harm, but it can't restore their power. They have bloodied their hands in vain, for the people of Oaxaca will not back down under this threat. It is said that Napoleon once observed that 'bayonets can be used for many purposes, but not to sit on'. This warning for amateur politicians has not been heard by Mexican political classes – not even after seeing the spectacular example of Iraq. With the army or the police you can destroy a country or a people but you cannot govern them.

AUGUST 1: THE REVOLUTION WILL BE TELEVISED
Confronted with the government's use of the media against the movement, several thousand women from APPO peacefully occupied the studios of the state radio and television network – after it refused to give them 15 minutes on the air. Through its outlets in Oaxaca, the media has continually been used by the governor to distribute propaganda against the movement. Now instead the occupiers of TV and radio stations disseminated the ideas, proposals, and initiatives of APPO. They also opened both radio and television for members of the public to express their own opinions 24 hours a day. Despite every imaginable technical difficulty (the women occupying the network had no previous training for this), thousands who called the stations made it onto the air. Eventually, a group of undercover police and mercenaries invaded the facilities, shooting up and destroying the equipment and injuring some of the APPO 'broadcasters'. In reaction, a few hours later APPO occupied all private radio and TV outlets in the city. Instead of one, APPO suddenly had 12 options to both disseminate information about the movement, and to give voice to the people. A few days later they gave the stations back to their owners, keeping only one powerful enough to cover the whole state. It broadcasted information about the movement 24 hours a day until it was jammed at the end of October.

RADICAL DEMOCRACY

APPO is the product of a slow accumulation of forces and many lessons gathered during previous struggles. In particular, three different democratic struggles have converged in the single one being waged by APPO. The first joins together all those who wish to strengthen formal democracy. People are tired of fraud and manipulation. The second gathers those who want a more participatory democracy. Besides transparency and honesty they want more civil involvement in the workings of government through the use of popular initiatives, referendums, plebiscites, the right to recall elected leaders, participatory budgeting, and other such tools. The third looks to extend and deepen autonomous or radical democracy. Eighty per cent of all municipalities in Oaxaca are indigenous and have their own particular, autonomous forms of government, following ancient traditions. Although this autonomy was legally recognised by Oaxaca's state law in 1995, it continues to be the subject of pressure and harassment. The advocates of radical democracy attempt now to invert this situation: to put the state and federal governments under pressure and harassment. The ultimate goal is to move from community and municipal autonomy to an autonomous coordination of groups of municipalities, from there to regions, and eventually to an autonomous form of government for the entire state. While this is an appeal to both sociological and political imaginations, it is also firmly based on legal and practical historical experience with autonomous self-government. Nor are the people of Oaxaca waiting for the inevitable departure of the governor to put these ideas into action; there are already many APPOs operating around the state on community, neighborhood, municipal, and regional levels. A group of lawyers is nourishing our dialogues and reflections with specific proposals for the new norms we will enact, transforming all public officers into public servants. The only authority will be the people themselves.

Oaxaca has already abolished its old, badly constituted state government. But there has never before been a 'crisis of governability'. In mid-September a violent brawl erupted during a private party in a neighborhood of Oaxaca. A half-drunk couple stumbled out onto the street. 'We should call the police,' he said. 'Don't be an ass,' she said, 'there are no police.' 'True,' he answered, scratching his head. 'Let's call APPO.'

'They're trying to force us to govern, but it's a provocation we're not going to fall for.' [*'Nos quieren obligar a gobernar. No caeremos en esa provocación.'*] This subtle bit of graffiti on a wall in Oaxaca reveals the nature of the present movement. It doesn't seek to take over the current power structure but to reorganise the whole of society from deep inside and establish new foundations for our social life together.

APPO cannot be reduced to a mere local disturbance or a rebellion. Rebellions are like volcanoes, mowing down everything before them. But they're also ephemeral; they may leave lasting marks, like lava beds, but they die down as quickly as they catch fire. They go out. And this one hasn't. In this case, the spirit of defiance has become too strong. Although Ulises Ruiz was the original focus of popular discontent he was just the detonator, the take-off point for a lasting movement of transformation to a peaceful, truly democratic society, for the harmonious coexistence of the different. As the Zapatista say, this is part of a struggle to create a world in which many worlds can be embraced. This is needed more than ever in a polarised society in which all forms of racism, sexism, individualism and violence are erupting.

THE END OF AN ERA

Fifty years ago Paul Goodman said:

> Suppose you had had the revolution you are talking and dreaming about. Suppose your side had won, and you had the kind of society you wanted. How would you live, you personally, in that society? Start living that way now! Whatever you would do then, do it now. When you run up against obstacles, people, or things that won't let you live that way, then begin to think about how to get over or around or under that obstacle, or how to push it out of the way, and your politics will be concrete and practical.

Thousands, millions of people assume now that the time has come to walk our own path. As the Zapatistas put it, to change the world is very difficult, if not impossible. A more pragmatic attitude demands the construction of a new world. That's what we are now trying to do, as if we had already won.

Ulises Ruiz appeared as a great obstacle. He incarnated the old world we wanted to get rid of. We thus provoked the collapse of his government. When the whole political system coalesced to support him, preventing his removal from office, we looked for alternatives. As Goodman suggested, we are finding ways to get over or around or under his police and his maneuvers. He can no longer govern but he daily organises shows for the media to pretend that he is still in charge. He cannot go anywhere in the state without a hundred bodyguards, protecting him from people's hostility. (The same is happening, by the way, with president Calderón. Even in Germany he needed to be protected by the police.)

We cannot wait for world revolution to dissolve the new forms of corporate capital. But we can attempt to make them marginal to our lives and to create new kinds of social relations. After refusing to be reduced to commodities and forced into alienated labour, after losing all the jobs many of us had, we are celebrating the freedom to work and we are renovating our old traditions of direct, non-exploitative exchange. We are thus enclosing the enclosers. And yes, we are winning, in spite of their violent reactions. Myriad initiatives are being launched in every corner of the state, offering solid proof of the vitality of the movement and people's ingenuity and courage.

We need, of course, all kinds of national and international solidarity. True, David can always win over Goliath if he fights him in his own territory, in his own way. But we cannot resist forever the daily aggression we are suffering, when every one of us is going to sleep, every night, not knowing if we will wake up in jail… or disappeared, or dead. But still, we are full of hope, smiling at the horror.

The time has come for the end of the economic era. Development, once a hope to give eternal life to economic societies, has instead dug their graves. Signs of the new era, though appearing everywhere, are still perceived as anomalies of the old. The old one, in turn, looks stronger than ever and the death it is carrying is still perceived as a symptom of vitality. If people are fooled by such images, disguised by slogans of the older period and remain blind to the evidence of the new era, the economy will continue to dismantle and destroy its own creations to the point of collapse.

There is an option. Now is the time for the option.

San Pablo Etla, January 2007

Gustavo Esteva is a prolific independent writer, a grassroots activist and a deprofessionalised intellectual based in Oaxaca, Mexico. He works both independently and in conjunction with a variety of Mexican NGOs and grassroots organisations and communities. In 1996, he was invited by the Zapatistas to be their advisor. Since then, he has been very active in what today is called *Zapatismo*, involving himself with the current struggle of the indigenous peoples, particularly with APPO. He can be contacted at gustavoesteva@gmail.com. For more on the Oaxaca uprising, check out www.oaxacalibre.org, www.oaxacarevolt.org, www.zmag.org and www.narconews. For more on the context of the movement and a connection with *Zapatismo*, see Esteva's article on zmag.org (http://www.zmag.org/content/showarticle.cfm?ItemID=11660). See also G. Esteva and M. Prakash, *Grassroots Postmodernism* (London: Zed Books, 1998).

Singularisation of the common

Thoughts on the crisis of the 'movement of movements'

Sandro Mezzadra and Gigi Roggero

OUR POINT OF DEPARTURE has to be the crisis – which is both a paradigmatic cipher of the present, but also an ambivalent situation, genealogically open and full of potentiality. When we try to move beyond a cyclical understanding of movements, we are not aiming to exclude the crisis from the horizon of possibility of political practice. Rather, the challenge is to situate the crisis in today's spatio-temporal coordinates. In fact, the difficulty of intervening in power relations, and the fact that the expansive possibilities of counter-summits have exhausted themselves, hasn't stopped the development of struggles: it may be enough to remember what happened last year in France, from the revolt in the *banlieues* to the remarkable movement against the CPE law, to realise how materially manifold and multiple the subjective web is, that bears the critique of the current condition. We could also recall the mobilisation of students and precarious workers in the Italian universities in the autumn of 2005, or the third transnational day of action on issues of migration on 7 October 2006; and last but not least, the everything-but-linear echo that the experiences of the EuroMayDay generated, which began to invent a new common vocabulary regarding work and precarity and which were initiated by activists from the space of the global movement. What does seem to have become smaller,

The CPE is the *Contrat Première Embauche*, roughly Contract of First Employment, according to which young people can be fired within a two-year period without explanation.

30

however, is the commonality, that – as we said – many of us thought we perceived between the revolt of Seattle 1999 and the worldwide mobilisation of 15 February 2003 against the Iraq war.

THE NEW CHALLENGES

So the crisis of the global movement poses a double challenge. The first aspect refers to the level on which the political practice of the movements is situated. Emerging from the opposition to neoliberal capitalism, they represented a different globalisation connected to the free circulation of people and knowledge, to social cooperation and struggles. Today we find that neoliberal politics are in a crisis, paradoxically symmetrical to that of the movements. This does not mean that the catastrophic effects of neoliberalism are over, only that such a politics can no longer solidify into a system. So the movements find themselves in an actual *post-neoliberal* scenario, precisely to the extent to which their political practice determined the crisis of neoliberalism and the impossibility of global government. The second aspect refers to the relationship between the new forms of movements in the last years and the radical transformations in the composition of labour-power and processes of production. There is no doubt that this relationship is rather problematic. Indeed, it is obvious, that – especially in Italy – the movements' difficulties in intervening in the relations of production marked a critical point of their developmental possibilities. However, those who criticise the movements' barriers with regard to the major fundamental or 'ethical' tasks should not ignore the fact that it is precisely this ethical dimension – of relations and language, of knowledge and affects – which is immanent to the new figures of living labour, today, when the entire spectrum of subjective resources and life itself are thrown into the labour process.

At the global level, meanwhile, the struggles of recent years – especially, although not exclusively, migrants' struggles – have shown the strategic relevance of conflicts around the control of mobility. Here runs the line demarcating autonomy and subjection, the fine line on which the class struggle is redefined at a transnational level. Must we not – restricting ourselves to Europe – in fact view the struggles of migration and precarity primarily from this perspective? There is of course no guarantee that migrants' struggles will converge with the struggles of the 'precarious' (a term that serves less and less to designate a particular segment of living labour today; it rather refers to the conditions that are currently in the process of becoming-common). Or better: the space of their convergence is not given by the 'objective' features that today mark the functioning of the capitalist mode of production. It has to be *politically constructed and conquered*. At the same time, experiences of tensions and conflicts accumulate, in different ways, within migration and precarity, signifying a historic phase in which mobility has become a decisive factor in the development of work, civil society, and forms of life. So it is not a coincidence that in the last few years it has been especially around these two topics that the most interesting forms of political practice and debate have developed in the European movements.

This is how it was possible to constitute connections and linkages allowing many activists to pass through the crisis of the global movement.

THE PROBLEM OF ORGANISATION

Having said that, we don't want to claim that there is a linear development that started in Seattle and ended in the revolt in the *banlieues* and against the CPE. On the contrary, we have to be able to determine the ruptures and the points at which continuity dissolves. This means productively tackling the crisis of the movements in order to articulate at a different level their processes of subjectification. Today, the strategies of the counter-summits, even if they can once again develop a rather significant dynamic of collective mobilisation (as the preparations for the anti-G8 in Heiligendamm show), can on the one hand probably not be reproduced quantitatively, while on the other they are insufficient – both in terms of their language and their forms of political action – to further develop and strengthen the conflicts around migration and precarity. At the same time, unsolved problems continue to exist within the global movement, especially the problem of *forms of organisation*. Even if the dissolution of the movement into thousands of tiny trickles, for example in Italy, has generated a certain identitarian reterritorialisation of different militant groups, we must not make the opposite mistake of being blinded by an aestheticised imaginary of deterritorialisation or a chimera-like nomadism that is incapable of becoming constituent power. At the same time there is the danger of merely repeating like a mantra obvious banalities: the argument that the party model, resting on a traditional relationship between vanguard and masses, has definitely run its course; or that the new form of cooperation, whether in production or in political practice, is the network.

The problem is that the network model itself is being practised today in a rather 'weak' form, rather than treating it as a powerful – and reproducible – organisational principle, capable of giving a political answer to the dissolution of the vanguard function in the living body of struggles. Take the example of EuroMayDay, whose importance and innovative power we have already highlighted. However, EuroMayDay did not manage to go beyond an expressive and clear suggestion regarding the question of self-representation of the 'precariat' on the European level. It primarily formed a kind of hub through which the explosive images were transmitted and the different parades met. In short, EuroMayDay did not manage to generate common forms of organisation and praxis, and thus become trigger, engine and catalyst of the struggles of living labour today, the principle of a new conflictuality and a political practice beyond the simultaneously manifest and unsolved crisis of representation.

MOVEMENT AND INSTITUTIONS

Another unsolved problem of the crisis of the global movement is the relationship of *movements to institutions*. In the spatio-temporal dimension of the global movement there were innovative and courageous attempts in this respect, but they seem to have disappeared with the crisis of the movement. In Italy, for example, the story, in short, went like this: a situation where parties of the institutional Left acted within the movement turned into one where important people from the movement ultimately retreated to institutional positions while the movement as a whole was not able to affect the mechanisms of government at different levels. Finally, once plunged into the abyss of the crisis of representation, the retreat of the parties of the Left to moderate positions, all the way to open rupture with the social movements, ended up compromising the very possibility of a new form of institutional politics – in the past it would have been called 'reformism'. The struggles have definitely – and luckily – shattered linearity in the relationship movement-parties-institutions, this pattern in which the movements supply the cues, pose the questions to which the political system supplies the answers, thus constituting itself as representative of all levels of society. In this way a new form of politics from within the institutions can – this becomes obvious here – under no circumstances conceive of its own relationship to the movements through the traditional imaginary of 'translation'. Put differently, its condition of possibility today is the necessary autonomy of the social movements. This precondition not only concerns the relationship of movements to the 'formal' institutions, it also applies to the capacity of the movements themselves to create their own institutions that – rather than stifle their growth – secure their reproduction, their development. Their capacity, to say it once more, to assert themselves within a common space.

LABORATORY LATIN AMERICA

So there's an insistent and urgent problem, that of the irreducible distance between the autonomy of the movements and the representative institutions that reproduce themselves despite the crisis: recognised institutions, one might say, although they seem to have lost their value (in other words, in spite of the fact that they seem less and less capable of manufacturing consensus and securing legitimacy and effectiveness for governmental action). We therefore need a new beginning, theoretically and practically, starting from the surplus of subjectivities and the conflicts with the political system and the institutional Left. For this we might have to once again change our focus and ditch the idea – both historicist and grounded in modernisation theory – that it is the role of the 'occident' to present to the 'Third World' its destiny as if in a mirror, whether with respect to capitalist development or revolutionary processes. The *laboratory Latin America* (as we summarily refer to the political and social processes of transformation that have recently stretched from Argentina to Venezuela, from Bolivia to Brazil) supplies not only starting points, if only situated and contradictory, for theoretical reflection, but actual elements of political models of the relationship between movements, governance and institutions. The point is not to cast an uncritical view on this laboratory, not to overlook the difficulties, contradictions and dead ends of both 'institutional' developments and dynamics of movement. Still, we can see here how the movements and struggles, which also in Latin America precede institutional attempts, continuously constitute and reproduce within themselves a field of possibilities. The point is that, from the insurrection in Venezuela 1989 to the revolt in Argentina 2001, from the struggles of the landless and workers in the *ABC paulista* in Brazil to those of the indigenous and miners in Bolivia, Latin America saw the composition of forces that in many cases managed to penetrate the interior of the political system. In Latin America there exists today within and outside of the institutions a constellation of subjectivities that, even if with a thousand contradictions, is working to disarticulate the institutions themselves and to open them for a process of emergence and consolidation of elements of *counter-power*. This opens the perspective of continually keeping open a constitutive basis that gives a new meaning to the institutions, anchors within them the movements' capacity to act continuously, and enables them to assert and maintain their autonomy. The continental horizon of many of the political projects there (beginning with *Bolivarismo*) at the same time continuously calls into question the reference to the nation as the privileged political horizon of the development of projects of political and social change. One could say that there is no spatial reference to the nation – even if it is present in official rhetoric – but to the two levels metropolis and continent, for it is these that are the loci of political practice as such. Maybe the laboratory Latin America only supplies 'suggestions'. Their meaning however seems to us uncontestable, their material basis are the remarkable struggles of the last years that span the whole continent.

THE DEFICITS IN EUROPE

Unfortunately as of yet nothing like this has happened in Europe. The movements did not manage to transform Europe into a place of conflict that would come closer to the global level. Still, the rejection of the EU constitution in France and the Netherlands prevented a Europe created 'from above'. So from both sides it is impossible to articulate at the European level a simultaneously conflictual and innovative relationship between movements and institutions as the result of substantial deficits on both sides. This is also why it's difficult to create a politics that would in fact – in its materiality, not only as a matter of principle – be transnational. In short: political practice today is no longer confined to the spatio-temporal *dispositif* of the nation-state, the struggles plunged the old top-down forms of government into the crisis, they are irrevocably gone. Today, *governance* – as a multilayered system of regulation, polycentric and with variable geometry – is the new terrain of conflict. On this terrain, demands are made and claims articulated: here the constitutive praxis of the autonomy of movements is developed.

FROM THE SPACE OF POLITICISATION...

Ultimately, three years on, the thesis that understands the movement as an open and complex space of politicisation seems to us both necessary and insufficient. Necessary, because it allowed us to recognise the material experience of having

created a *common place* in the practice of the global movement – that which was incommensurable and qualitatively new in comparison to the sum of the parts of which the movement was composed. Within the movement, social subjectivities went beyond traditional organisations which, on the other hand, – at least for a short time – took on supportive roles. That was the space in which the *multitude* became flesh: it had been theoretically described in the long winter of the 1990s, now it became flesh and blood in the streets of Seattle and Genoa. The term multitude proves to be convincing when the point is to understand the insurrection of subjectivities at the level of the common while leaving behind both the liberal religion of the individual and the socialist cult of the collective. The ambivalent relationship of individual and state, of private and public, of citizenry and nation is finally broken. Instead there materialises a process of singularisation in the common; or rather, in the conflict there is created that 'common place' that does not demand the sacrifice of the exploited singularities of which living labour is composed today. On the contrary, the cooperative and innovative capacity, the practice of freedom based on equality, is multiplied. In this, the point is to investigate more closely the relationship of class and multitude to keep in focus the paths and struggles of mobile and flexible labour and not become separated from their materiality.

...TO THE SPACE OF ORGANISATION

The thesis is insufficient, however, because the movement only hinted at the radical questions and the orientation of political practice, highlighted both of these primarily negatively, while it was not able to find positive answers. To claim that the key task is no longer the conquest of state power runs the risk of remaining with a weak diagnosis that was already valid before the Zapatista insurrection renewed many of the communicative and linguistic codes of radical politics. Once again: it is the struggles that are primary, and indeed it was the movements of the 1960s and 1970s that realised that exodus away from state power. Now however, the point is to talk about a new necessity in the spatio-temporal *dispositif* of the movements: the transition from the space of politicisation and subjectification to the space of organisation. How can the changes form a sediment, how can power relations be affected, how can the opening and development of a constitutive space, a common, be secured? In other words, how can one employ the relations of power without 'taking power'?

To these questions, that much is clear, we have no answers. We believe that the movements and the struggles of the next years have to discover these. In conclusion we would like to restrict ourselves to a simple proposition. Italian labour law recognises a type of contract called *Lavoro a progetto* – 'project-based employment' – a type that obviously constitutes a relationship of precarious labour. The point is now to invert this meaning, to suggestively appropriate it in order to operate with it within the crisis of representation. In other words: in those areas where the movement was able to agitate and have an impact – from migration to precarity, from questions of the welfare state to those of income – the point is to create forms of project-representation that open a space for experiments and conflicts with the institutions and the 'official' representative subjects (parties and unions) based on flexible relationships and a variable geometry, so that the autonomy of movements remains intact and the irreducible distance in relation to the political system is extended. The autonomy of the movements has to pass through the crisis of representation. Only then does it seem possible to us to imagine reaching beyond it to a non-state public sphere, to finally a common.

Translated from the German by Tadzio Müller and Ben Trott

Sandro Mezzadra and Gigi Roggero were editors of *DerriveApprodi* and co-authored the text 'Luoghi Comuni' (Common Places – available at http://www.generation-online.org/t/deriveapprodi.htm). Gigi is active in Uninomade and the European Precarity Web Ring project and lives in Rome. Sandro lives in Bologna and is active in migration issues with the Frassanito network. This article originally appeared in German (translated from the Italian original by Thomas Atzert) in *Fantomas* #10.

A new weather front

Paul Sumburn

AFTER YEARS of drawing attention to the facts of climate change, suddenly the issue is everywhere, and everyone, it seems, is calling for action to reduce greenhouse gas emissions. In some senses this is a rare victory, a response both to the pressure of activists and the scientific consensus channelled powerfully by the United Nation's Intergovernmental Panel on Climate Change. But, of course, some see the potential to expand the sphere of capital's influence: most mainstream talk is of market-friendly technological solutions, 'carbon trading' and oil companies dabbling in renewable energy.

This new situation raises important questions about strategy. It's no longer about making a noise and raising the issue: it's about getting to grips with the fundamental problem. In the UK the growing movement against the fossil fuel economy has attempted to find a way out of this rhetorical labyrinth by taking action that stops or reduces carbon dioxide emissions whilst promoting workable ecological solutions and challenging dominant power structures. First we describe what we did, and second we describe how climate change, capitalism and resistance to both, all fit together.

THE CAMP FOR CLIMATE ACTION

In August 2006 around 600 people worried about climate change, and looking for something beyond the empty rhetoric of the politicians and corporations, got together for a two week camp next to the UK's largest power station and tried to shut it down. The focus of the camp was power. Drax coal-fired power station provides around 7% of the UK's electricity and produces over 20 million tons of CO_2 each year. Its existence and continued use is incompatible with any kind of ecological or equitable future. Our attempts to shut it down were an audacious strike both at a source of CO_2 emissions and a lynchpin of 21st century capitalism.

The camp embodied three key ideas. First, a commitment to direct action: a belief that solutions to the problem of climate change lie not with governments and corporations but with grassroots movements for change. On the day of action the camp attempted to breach the power station perimeter with the aim of occupying the site and closing it down. On this occasion we didn't achieve our objectives (due in part to the massive security operation involving 4,000 police) although the role of coal, the dirtiest fossil fuel, was exposed for the first time. Second, a commitment to popular education. The camp was a site for over 100 meetings and workshops, on climate and related issues. Finally we experimented with alternatives to the social relations of capitalism. The camp was organised as an autonomous space, from eating to entertainment to satellite-linked internet connections, with decisions made via non-hierarchical methods of consensus and a strong commitment to limiting our environmental impact. Many of the ideas for the camp's organisation came from a re-creation of the 'neighbourhood' or *barrio* system of organisation as used in 2002 at the Strasbourg no border camp and continued in 2005 at the G8 camp in Stirling, Scotland. This commitment to autonomy, non-hierarchy and low impact living inspired many for whom the camp was their first experience of political activity.

BEYOND GREENWASH

There is a remarkable mismatch between rhetoric and reality when it comes to climate change. The attempt to reengineer reality in terms of market solutions is about more than presentation and image, it's a modal shift in the market to fend off the growth in more radical and threatening ideas (ones that suggest the market is in fact the problem). As one would expect the oil companies are out there at the forefront of this latest wave of greenwash. BP is for example planning a new gas-fired, zero-emission power station in Scotland that buries all its waste CO_2 far below the North Sea, thus in their words taking hundreds of thousands of car equivalents of the roads. Further down we find out that the buried CO_2 is actually being used to help pump out otherwise unreachable oil reserves releasing millions of new barrels of oil that – surprise surprise – will put many more cars back on the road than the first sleight of hand is taking off. Calling BP 'Beyond Petroleum' is like calling the British Army 'Beyond Violence'. The oil companies will drill every last barrel of oil and gas there is on this planet until and unless they are stopped. Meanwhile the UK government talks green in one corner with a climate change bill (tying the government to binding targets for emissions reductions) but in the other corner it promotes road building, aviation expansion, free trade, and a relaxation of planning laws in favour of big developers.

The camp was in many ways a great success but any temporary gathering of people has its limitations and important strategic questions remain. Many of us organising the camp recognised how the summit gatherings met our crucial need for convergence, for coming together and acting in unison. We also rejected the over-emphasis on individual responsibility and wanted to take on the corporate interests which cause large emissions and which can only be tackled through collective effort. It's important that, where they can, people make individual changes but switching light bulbs doesn't connect a person with real causes of climate change, the political and economic system. We felt that the climate camp could learn from summit convergences, but also had the potential to move beyond them in a number of ways. First, the camp was at a time and place of our choosing. One of the dangers of the G8 gatherings is that we become an institutionalised symbolic mirror. They have their summit; we try to stop it. The climate camp, for some, was an attempt to break out of that cycle.

Second, the camp was a direct attempt to stop something real, in this case a power station and CO_2 emissions. Symbolic action can be, and has been, profoundly important but there is a danger that summit gatherings are increasingly lost in a hall of mirrors. Over time the symbolism of our protest is drained of its power. There is, of course, a risk that the climate camp could itself create new false targets as people imagine that Drax (or any similar place) is capitalism and not just a large machine animated by capitalist process.

Finally, the camp was also an attempt to challenge the pessimism around this issue. Faced with the full facts about climate change and the massive reduction in emissions necessary over a very short period of time, it's all too easy to either deny the problem or conclude that it's too late, that it's an issue so large and entrenched that it's without solution. We found it remarkable that scientists' predictions of global catastrophe under business-as-usual had hardly animated radicals. We wanted to move away from denial. We wanted to say that the future is, literally, in our hands.

THE OSTRICH HAS LEFT THE BUILDING

Ostriches were a recurring motif of the camp. Publicity posters showed people with heads in the sand and at one point during the demonstrations the police confiscated a giant puppet of an ostrich, suspecting it contained equipment for direct action. But the figure of the ostrich no longer captures the problem before us. Climate change is no longer being ignored but that doesn't mean that we can move on.

We have to realise that capitalism may not have to sort climate change out in order to survive. Or at least it might need to avoid only the very highest of the projected temperature rises. It's important to remember that capitalism operates by breaking down and collapsing. It contracts through war, depression or restructuring in order to allow for a new round of growth. In fact it has already written off large parts of the world as surplus populations. The most likely scenario is a version of business as usual with some attempts to ameliorate conditions for a much smaller guaranteed core, alongside a huge increase in securitisation against the rest of the world. The only check on this nightmare is what we, as local and world population, will put up with. We could even say that the temperature of the earth will be a measure of our ability to self-organise. Literally keeping the earth within liveable temperatures will be the definition of the success or failure of class struggle in the 21st century.

There is a fundamental difference between the levels of climate change that those who make the rules, make investment decisions, and the like are happy to accept, and the levels that peasant farmers, slum-dwellers and factory workers can tolerate. What's 'dangerous' for the former are changes in the weather that cause international security problems (as the UK government made clear in its presentation to the UN Security Council made clear) and changes in the weather that, domino-like, cause a massive contraction of the economy (as the UK government's Stern report sets out). What's 'dangerous' to the latter are crop failure and hunger, destroyed houses from extreme rains and storms, and everywhere across the Third World, heatstrokes and exhaustion, primarily affecting the young, old, and ill.

BIOLOGICAL PRECARITY AND CLASS-BASED WEATHER FRONTS

Climate change takes many of the major problems, tragedies and dilemmas we currently face and acts as a multiplier. People are dying of starvation now; climate change will add many millions more. There are refugees now, and environmental refugees already outnumber those displaced by armed conflict, according to the Red Cross, yet climate change will change rainfall patterns, causing mass ecological dislocation and migration as some places become agriculturally dead. At the beginning of the 21st century weather is the frontline in the conflict between rich and poor, between west and south, between one class and another.

Remember Katrina? Remember the gridlocked highways as the wealthy escaped the city leaving the poor behind to face the hurricane? Credible scientific predictions suggest that unless emissions are drastically reduced, the synthesis of global temperature rise and precarity (or precariousness) will cause the mass-migrations of hundreds of millions of people and food shortages in rich countries. Given our socially interconnected world this could be the making of a revolution, or make the

Let's be clear, it is the wealthy that produce most CO_2 emissions. That goes for countries and individuals within countries. In the UK we produce on average around 9 tons of CO_2 per head of population compared to a Tanzanian who produces around 0.1 tons. Within the UK it is the wealthy who drive and fly most. The world economy is built on the self-expansion of alienated labour but the burning of fossil fuels has also been intrinsic to industrial expansion, providing energy for the machines that labour uses. Shifting weather patterns are not a form of direct control, like military invasion or economic constraint, but they exacerbate the already appalling divisions between rich and poor.

tragedies of the twentieth century appear mild. Again, this will be down to people's choices. Climate change is the vicious end result of an international class war that started with slavery and imperialism and is now manifest as neoliberal globalisation. The question to us is where will it end?

There is no such thing as a 'natural disaster'. The impacts of extreme natural events form a tragic map of inequality, disadvantage and class division. The wealthy have better housing and live in safer places. When things go wrong they have access to better health care and the finances to start again. On looking at who is affected worst by earthquakes in the South, some geographers now describe them as 'class quakes'. Climate change is no different, except in terms of scale. It's the poor who live on the banks of rivers and estuaries that might flood, whose housing is most vulnerable to storms, who are the first to starve when food prices rise and who have limited means to rebuild when things go wrong. On top of this existing economic and social precarity, the exhaust fumes of neoliberalism, in the form of climate change, are ushering in a new era of biological precarity.

THERE IS ONLY ENVIRONMENT

To get to grips with this mess we need to move beyond the green movement's tendency to construct the environment as a separate sphere or as an idealised moral good. Enclosure of the natural world is seen as an unfortunate and curable symptom of the market rather than one of its fundamental and necessary modes of expansion. We can also see how climate change, like human rights, may be turned around and

used against us. Just as humanitarian intervention has been used as a mask for power politics, such as justifying the invasion of Iraq, environmentalism may suffer the same fate. In fact the process is well underway. In the Lacondon jungle of Chiapas, southern Mexico the government is attempting to 'resettle' communities that are now in zones designated for conservation. This is because there is a grand plan, the Plan Puebla Panama, to 'develop' (i.e. enclose) Central America. Conservationists kicked up a fuss and were granted the Mesoamerican Biological Corridor, a conservation initiative. So the local people are now in the 'wrong' place. This isn't simply a case of spin by the Mexican government: one of the prime movers behind this has been the giant US eco-NGO Conservation International, which worked intimately with the military and Mexican government to design the reserve areas. The indigenous people have done a good job of preserving their local environment – so much so that it's globally important for conservation – yet if we consider only the environment then we end up siding with the Mexican military and against the Zapatistas.

What this makes clear is that we can't treat climate change as a separate issue: like everything else, power relations run right through it. Any movement based around climate change has to be enmeshed in the rest of the problems of the world's movements. Likewise any movement for a liveable future needs to take on climate change. Climate change is not a cause; it's a symptom (albeit one with the potential to kill off the patient). Equally the impacts and interconnectedness of climate change will undermine any success we might have in other areas. In the context of the debate in these pages it will be difficult to talk of winning, as millions starve or the Amazon burns. Looking at it this way round, we can see that climate change has the potential to link us not just as victims of disaster but as people fighting together.

COMMON STRUGGLE
As we've already hinted, the links between radical campaigning on climate change and other areas are so strong that they could in time become indivisible. Migration is one key example: the greatest cause of migration in coming years will be climate change-induced drought and 'natural' disasters. We must say yes to a world without borders, and equally yes to people having a functioning environment wherever they choose to live. We sometimes neglect to look at the causes of migration because we don't want to reduce our focus on the injustice of border control and racist immigration policy. Unless we act now, the near future will see a world in which people are forced to migrate in vastly increased numbers and in which fear-induced border policy becomes more extreme.

Whilst the struggle against alienating, shit work is an essential measure of our struggles against capitalism, it is also essential for solving the problem of carbon emissions. Capital's main means of winning out in workplace struggles is either attack, restructuring and increasing precarity, or else paying people off with increased wages. In neither case is the central issue of exploitation challenged. Instead the globalised (and thus increasingly energy-intensive) nature of capital is affirmed. In the former, capital is globalised to weaken the position of the worker; in the latter the worker strikes a kind of deal with the devil and accepts an increased level of consumption in return for ongoing alienation. Both options exacerbate climate change.

In an increasingly globalised market the chances are that what we produce has an ever more remote relationship to our actual needs. A growth in consumption is both the market's solution and its *raison d'être*. But how do workers take back meaning and control? Part of this must involve autonomy but part must also mean relocalisation. Of course local production is not sufficient to solve the problem of alienation and exploitation (there are countless 'local' businesses that are as corrupt and exploitative as those keyed into global markets). But at the same time autonomy alone is not enough. While there is a world of difference between worker control and capitalist control, shit and polluting work remains shit and polluting work, regardless of who owns the production line. Our challenge is to tackle both the relationships within the workplace and the kind of work being done. In other words solutions to climate change have to encourage good solutions to crap work: not more consumption and exploitation but less work and commodities and more free time and happiness.

Moreover climate change makes us all potentially precarious because it undermines the ways people try to achieve security within capitalism. A climate-related economic crash is a growing possibility, given the increasing frequency of extreme weather events and the impact of this on both infrastructure and the insurance industry. This crash alone won't necessarily undermine capitalism but it will wipe out pensions, house prices, savings etc. We've seen in Argentina how precarious those forms of security are.

There is a danger of a vicious circle emerging, with the atomisation and conflict being caused by the huge increase in precarity then feeding back into support for

There's no doubt that a social movement with climate change as one of its central concerns is the only way to tackle human-induced climate change and the expansion of capital. The Climate Camp is an active part of that movement and a place where it can constitute itself. Climate change and the growing rhetoric around it expose a crack in the system. While the mainstream attempts to plaster this over with techno-fixes, there is, at the same time, the chance to expose the limits of these solutions and turn people on to the need for more fundamental action. The vast political space opened up by climate change will either be filled by business people and industry selling the latest shiny, plastic, bury-it, green-it, burn-it, offset-it, sell-it solutions or by people who have a critique of capitalism and can see enclosure and intensification as both an inevitable expression of capital and a changeable reality. There's going to be a climate camp from 14 to 21 August 2007, celebrating these possibilities and challenging the fossil fuel economy not by 2030 or 2050, not upon a timeline set by the market but in the here and now. So if you can, come and join us for some serious climate action. www.climatecamp.org.uk

Money for nothing?

Max Henninger

ONE OF THE STRATEGIC PROPOSALS most widely debated within contemporary political movements opposing capitalist globalisation is that for a basic income de-linked from wage labour. Various French and Italian theorists have contributed significantly to spreading awareness of this proposal. Its history within the radical Left of the Federal Republic of Germany (FRG) is less well known. The following remarks are a modest attempt to consider that history and its implications for those advocating a basic income today. The conclusions drawn are derived exclusively from the German situation. Whether or not they also hold for other countries is a question the reader must decide for him- or herself.

THE BASIC INCOME PROPOSAL IN THE FRG
In the FRG, the demand for a basic income was first formulated following the 1981/82 economic crisis and the 1982 chancellorship of Helmut Kohl, the conservative politician who remained in power until after the annexation of the German Democratic Republic (1990). At the time, the proposal to introduce a basic income was advanced by political organisations fending for the rights of welfare recipients. It was a response to rising unemployment and the austerity measures championed by Kohl. The proposal never became part of a widely endorsed militant platform, largely remaining a matter of theoretical debate instead. This was still evident in 1998, when a congress devoted to the basic income was organised by autonomist activists in Berlin. The congress was relatively well attended and kept the theoretical debate alive, but it did not lead to significant changes in what was then already a highly fragmented militant practice.

In 2005, the basic income resurfaced as one of several demands formulated by the organisers of the weekly 'Monday demonstrations' held throughout the FRG. These demonstrations, attended mainly by the country's unemployed, protested the austerity and workfare measures currently being implemented in Germany. Like earlier germs of popular resistance, the Monday demonstrations have not developed into a broad militant movement. Nevertheless, the basic income proposal is currently being debated more widely in the FRG than it has been for years. It features on the platform of the German section of Attac as well as in the programs of several regionally and nationally organised extra-parliamentary groups. Some members of the reformist Left Party are fending for the basic income in parliament. Variants of the proposal are also being debated within the academy, mostly by representatives of the liberal or centre-left spectrum such as sociologists Ulrich Beck and Claus Offe. Entrepreneurs (Goetz Werner) and neoliberal economists (Thomas Straubhaar) have also recently jumped on the bandwagon. This development has of course provoked fierce polemics as to how progressive the basic income proposal really is.

As defined by the Basic Income Earth Network (BIEN), the basic income would be a monetary sum paid out to every citizen on a regular (e.g. monthly) basis, regardless of that citizen's employment history and his or her reliance on other incomes. The basic income would be sufficient for financing a comfortable standard of living, and it would be paid out regardless of the recipient's financial situation. Radical proponents of the basic income insist on the need for de-linking it from every obligation to work, whereas liberal proponents tend to view it as a way of remunerating various forms of nonprofit community service, which they would make compulsory. Models for financing the basic income range from the so-called 'take half model' (which proposes a 50% tax on every income, regardless of its magnitude) and a dramatic increase in value-added tax to various forms of progressive taxation. Some have also proposed a tax on financial transactions.

Several proponents of the basic income consider it an adequate replacement for the various forms of financial support currently administered by the FRG's welfare state. Others envision it as a supplement to such support. There is a consensus among the basic income's proponents that the FRG's welfare state is inadequate in its present form, and that it is currently suffering a serious crisis. A brief consideration of the phenomena underlying this view is indispensable for properly evaluating the basic income proposal.

CLASS DECOMPOSITION

In the FRG as in other countries, official statements about the welfare state's growing difficulties in financing its services (pensions, public healthcare, and unemployment relief) can be heard daily. Such statements have recently been used to justify both the raising of the legal pension age from 65 to 67 years and a significant increase in value-added tax. They have also been used to justify reforms that increase the pressure on unemployed persons to return to work while exposing those persons to a number of humiliating measures such as unannounced house visits. Many of the long-term unemployed are now being forced to move into smaller, less costly apartments.

Understanding these developments requires recognition of some basic facts about the welfare state and its function within capitalist economies. The most important thing to recognise is that the welfare state does not in any meaningful sense pay for the survival of the economically needy. In the case of pensions, the state merely appropriates a percentage of the wages of full-time workers and promises to return this sum after those workers are no longer of use on the labour market. Unemployment relief is also financed out of the wages of full-time workers. This strict correlation between waged labour and the sums made available for survival in old age or during unemployment has important consequences. How much an entrepreneur pays into the welfare fund depends on the number of full-time workers he or she employs. This creates an incentive to reduce the number of such workers by downsizing, outsourcing, and relocating production to countries with more attractive systems of taxation. It also creates an incentive to resort to part-time work, temp work, and internships.

The pension system delegates responsibility for financing the survival of one part of the non-working population to other parties (entrepreneurs and workers). The state appropriates funds through political constraint, without entering into a formal contract with those from whom it appropriates them. This means the conditions for money being paid out in the form of pensions can be altered at any time (by lowering pensions, either directly or by raising taxes, and by raising the legal pension age). The same is true of unemployment relief, as illustrated by the recent changes both in the criteria by which eligibility is determined and in the magnitude of the sums paid out, and it is also true of the public healthcare system. The latter forces the working population to cover its own healthcare costs even when those costs result from entrepreneurial or state decisions (as is the case, for example, with costs resulting from environmental pollution or war).

The welfare state is premised on the hegemony of a particular type of employment relation, that of the full-time worker. This worker is essentially the male, Fordist worker championed by the traditional labour movement. Where this employment relation becomes less widespread, the welfare state quickly runs into difficulties. The tendential waning of the Fordist employment relation is one of the root causes of the welfare state's current crisis. This crisis is genuine despite the ideological smokescreens surrounding it.

Between 1991 and 2005, the number of employment relations in Germany corresponding to the model of the full-time worker who pays into the pension, healthcare, and unemployment funds declined by 13%. In absolute terms, the number of workers in such employment relations – still characterised as 'normal' in German economic discourse – sank from about 30 to about 26 million. About 30% of German workers now find themselves in so-called 'atypical' employment relations, such as part-time or temp work, with 23% of the working population doing part-time work. Most of these part-time workers are employed in so-called 'Minijobs' or 'Midijobs'. This means they earn a maximum of €400 or €800 a month, respectively. Neither they nor their employers pay into the pension fund. Many such workers do not have healthcare.

In addition to these developments, low wages have become increasingly widespread throughout the FRG, even among those employed full-time. Both nominal and real wages have been sinking consistently since the mid-1990s. This further reduces the magnitude of the sums available for redistribution by the welfare state. A growing number of qualified workers and persons with a higher education are affected by the drop in wages, as are workers above the age of 30. Women are especially hard hit, as they make up about 70% of workers in the service sector, where wages have traditionally been low. German trade unions have frequently sanctioned the fixing of low wage standards in the service sector, as in Saxony, where the standard wage for hairdressers is now €3.06 an hour. The pressure on wages (and the incentive to sack 'normal' full-time workers) has been increased significantly by the introduction of workfare measures such as the 'one-euro-jobs' championed by former chancellor Gerhard Schroeder. This measure allows entrepreneurs to recruit unemployed persons for a purely symbolic wage of €1, for up to 150 hours a month.

Comparing the FRG's current labour market with that of the early 1970s, when the country's radical Left began borrowing the concept of 'class composition' from Italian theorists, one is tempted to characterise the developments just described as 'class decomposition'. During the early 1970s, the strength of the German welfare system rested on the figure of the Fordist worker championed by the traditional labour movement. Today, this worker – who never represented the entirety or even the most exploited sector of the working class, but was arguably important by virtue of the political power he exerted by means of the trade unions – is threatening to become a marginal figure. He is tendentially yielding to a plethora of persons in highly diverse and unstable employment relations. They do not dispose of the reliable and comparatively high income the traditional welfare state administered and partially redistributed with relative success during its heyday (the years of 'full' – and full-time – employment between 1958 and 1975). A significant part of the working population is now excluded from the welfare state's services, just as many workers no longer provide that state with the funds it requires to operate successfully.

WHAT KIND OF PROPOSAL IS THE BASIC INCOME PROPOSAL?

The basic income proposal represents one possible way of addressing the crisis of the welfare state. When assessing this proposal, it is worth keeping in mind just what it is and what it is not. Within the radical Left, the basic income is associated with much rhetoric, but there is often little consideration of the sometimes ambivalent developments its implementation would entail.

The basic income proposal does not address the question of who owns and controls the means of production. This partly explains why those representatives of the FRG's capital-owning classes sufficiently sober-minded to recognise the problems faced by the welfare state have recently taken so warmly to the basic income. They have an interest in assuring not just the physical reproduction, but also the political quiescence of the labouring classes. The basic income promises both. Many models for financing the basic income also present entrepreneurs with the prospect of significant fiscal relief. This is the case, for example, with the 'take half' model. Furthermore, the introduction of a basic income would facilitate a dramatic lowering of wages. If the basic income were to be financed by an increase in value-added tax, this would allow entrepreneurs to continue shifting the burden of financing the reproduction of the wage- and welfare-dependent classes onto those classes themselves.

This is related to another feature of the proposal, which is that it is focused on circulation, rather than on production. The basic income is a device for re-distributing existing incomes – or, more generally, economic value. It does not address the question of how economic value is produced. This has significant consequences. If the basic income were to be financed by a tax on entrepreneurial profits, this would create a strong incentive for the corporations affected to increase those profits – a development that would not necessarily affect the recipients of the basic income in the country where it is introduced, but which would have significant consequences for workers in the countries where the corporations on whom the tax is levied produce. One of the corporations affected in the FRG, for example, would be Volkswagen, which now produces mainly in Slovakia. When the German radical Left demands the introduction of a basic income in the FRG, to be financed by a tax on entrepreneurial profits, it is implicitly demanding increased exploitation in countries such as Slovakia.

This is one, but not the only sense in which the basic income proposal is tendentially nationalist, and perhaps even racist. By appealing to national governments for legal and economic reform, the proponents of the basic income implicitly recognise the legitimacy of the nation state. They thereby tacitly accept the criteria by which national governments grant or refuse a person the status of legal citizen. A law introducing a basic income for all citizens of the FRG would simultaneously refuse such an income to all undocumented immigrants, regardless of the fact that these immigrants and their off-the-books labour are an important part of the FRG's economy.

Arguably, this nationalist or racist element of the proposal entails a sexist element. As noted, many persons who depend for their living on labour performed in the lower strata of the service sector are women. A significant number of these women are also undocumented immigrants. The introduction of a basic income would improve the financial situation of most middle-class households, but it would not alter the situation of the many female undocumented immigrants who perform domestic work in those households. Some German proponents of the basic income have suggested the implementation of their proposal would allow women to withdraw from the labour market and concentrate on housework and childrearing. In making such statements, they are ignoring those women who are not recognised as legal citizens and would therefore not be eligible for a basic income. They are also contributing to the anti-feminist rollback the country has been experiencing for several decades. The protagonists of that rollback defend a similarly reactionary concept of female identity.

It may be objected that no fundamentally nationalist and sexist system allows for implementing reforms in a way that is not to some extent complicit in this nationalism and sexism, however radical those reforms may otherwise be. If this is true (and there is much to suggest it is), the question becomes whether or not one wants to be actively involved in such reformism. Ultimately, this is a question politically active individuals and groups need to settle for themselves. It is difficult to make general prescriptions. Not only do the data currently available allow for divergent projections about likely future developments, but the decision would also seem to partly be a question of personal morality. What can be said, however, is that possible effects of a basic income such as the further institutionalisation of racism and sexism should not be ignored.

Since the basic income proposal brackets the question of who owns and controls the means of production, it should be clear that it is reformist in the sense that it accepts many basic parameters of developed capitalist economies. Far from eliminating the social relation that capitalism is, a relation that finds its clearest expression in the wage and in the money form in general, the basic income proposal in fact depends on and accommodates itself to that relation. While it certainly represents a particularly extreme device for redistributing incomes through taxation, such redistribution is far from being new to capitalism or incompatible with it.

One last feature of the basic income proposal worth emphasising is its profoundly voluntarist character. The history of the proposal in the FRG shows it has been endorsed only by relatively narrow sectors of the exploited classes, namely the unemployed and – more recently – those young, often academically qualified persons to whom the FRG's current labour market offers few possibilities besides internships, self-employment, and sporadic part-time or temp work. The basic income proposal has been consistently rejected by the FRG's organised workers, who are rightly distrustful of the tax measures by which its advocates hope to finance it. Proponents of the basic income often speak as if calls for such a measure might constitute the basis for a broadly endorsed militant platform. They can do so because the proposal addresses the economic insecurity and the desire for a liberation from work that are indeed characteristics shared by most members of the exploited classes. Yet in considering only questions of how value circulates, and not of how it is produced, these proponents of the basic income also gloss over the significant differences associated with the specific positions various kinds of workers and unemployed persons hold within the economy. The arguments formulated by these proponents of the basic income are voluntarist in that they conclude from the common predicament of being wage- or welfare-dependent that a political unity can be established regardless of the fact that economic exploitation and constraint take a variety of different forms, each entailing its own risks and privileges and giving rise to different, sometimes antagonistic interests.

Max Henninger lives and works in Berlin. He is co-editor, with Giuseppina Mecchia and Timothy S. Murphy, of 'Italian Post-Workerist Thought' (a special issue of the journal *Substance* devoted to the work of Antonio Negri, Paolo Virno, Antonella Corsani, and others) and author of 'Doing The Math: Reflections on the Alleged Obsolescence of the Law of Value under Post-Fordism' (*ephemera: theory and politics in organization*, 7.1).

Walking in the right direction?

Ben Trott

CRISIS

Neoliberalism is in crisis. It began, at the very latest, ten years ago with the collapse of the so-called Asian 'tiger economies' (Indonesia, Thailand, South Korea…). The protests surrounding the World Trade Organisation (WTO) Ministerial in Seattle two years later reflected its continuation and deepening. They not only catapulted the global movement into the limelight, but coincided with (and partly induced) the faltering of talks within the conference centre. For the neoliberal project, almost every round of multilateral trade negotiations that has followed has been similarly catastrophic: the Central American Free Trade Agreement, the Free Trade Area of the Americas (FTAA), the Doha Round of WTO negotiations… Further indexes as to the depth of the current crisis include: the 'No' vote on the EU constitution; the series of recent election victories in Latin America and beyond won on an anti-neoliberal ticket; and the response to the events of September 11, 2001, where the threat of an open-ended global war has finally demolished globalisation's promise of a more harmonious, inter-connected world.

Yet crisis is not necessarily cause for celebration. The East Asian financial crisis caused millions to fall below the poverty line and did little to strengthen the hand of labour. The collapse of multilateral trade talks have largely been the result of alliances between nation states (like the 'Group of 21' led by Brazil and India, formed at the WTO Minsterial in Cancún), acting in their own economic self-interest – or rather, that of their elite. Moreover, their demands have tended not to be anti-neoliberal *per se*, but rather for 'fair play' and the reciprocal opening of barriers in the North.

Similarly, the anti-neoliberal credentials of some of Latin America's newly elected presidents could be called into question. And the onset of a global state of exception, with the suspension of legal rights (supposedly, and paradoxically, in order to defend them), in the name of counter-terrorism certainly represents a particularly worrying turn. It is nonetheless important to recognise the role that the cycle of struggles which found its most prominent articulation in the events of Seattle and Genoa has played in bringing about the current crisis, and thus the role we have played as active subjects (rather than mere passive objects) in the making of the present.

Simultaneously, the 'movement of movements' finds itself in crisis too. We would seem to have run up against our own limits. The current cycle is drawing to an end; entering a 'downturn', if not necessarily quantitatively, then certainly qualitatively. The movements' beginnings (the time when 'we were winning') were characterised by a tremendous celebration of our 'unity in diversity'. Steelworkers were facing off riot cops, together with environmentalists dressed as sea turtles. Nuns were taking part in street protests alongside queer activists. Two slogans summed up the sentiment of the day, one coined before Seattle, one after. 'Walking,' the EZLN's ever-poetic Subcommandante explained, 'we ask questions.' A few years later, as if directly replying to Thatcher's T-I-N-A ('There Is No Alternative') maxim, the World Social Forum declared 'Another World Is Possible'. Notable about both slogans was the extent to which (despite rather 'orthodox' tendencies that remain within both groupings) they departed from the previous certainty of Marxist-Leninism. Whilst both implied the need to ask What Is to Be Done?, neither claimed to always already have the answer. However, a movement as broad and contradictory as ours was always going to have to ask (and try to answer): 'Walking where, actually?' and 'What sort of world?'

To the same extent that the crisis of neoliberalism should not necessarily be cause for celebration, the movement's own crisis should not – necessarily – be grounds for despair. To recognise the limits of a particular moment or phase of struggle does not have to imply an inability to move beyond them. Doing so, however, requires a willingness to engage in critical reflection, and an openness towards different forms and methods of political practice.

BEYOND UNITY

If the challenge, then, is to move beyond a relatively uncritical celebration of unity in diversity, without slipping back into the 'old' (tried, tested and failed) ways of doing things, surely the question is as follows: *How do we set in motion a process by which one group (most often, but not always, a party) is no longer able to dominate all the others, seeking to remake them in its own image; and where, at the same time, we are able to move beyond merely existing indifferently alongside each other?* This, of course, is not a question of internal movement organisation (although it is that as well): it is far more fundamental. How do we create what the Zapatistas have called 'a world in which many worlds are possible'?

Discussions have been taking place within the radical Left in Germany around precisely (if not exactly explicitly) this question. One possible solution which has begun to be formulated is the development of a set of so-called 'directional demands' (*Richtungsforderungen*). There is no single, unified position on what do or do not constitute directional demands. What follows should be understood more as an intervention into an ongoing discussion than as an introduction to a completed debate.

First and foremost, the deployment of directional demands represents the desire to constitute a social actor, movement or counter-power capable of intervening in, and influencing, social and political developments. The objective is the generalisation of common anti-capitalist struggles. In other words, to bring about a class recomposition – with class here defined not in the traditional narrow sense of (male) industrialised workers, but as the irreducible multiplicity of singular subjectivities involved in creative, productive social activity. It is an effort to contribute to the process of breaking with capitalist social relations, through engaging and connecting with social struggles – rather than remaining on the level of abstract, sloganeering radicalism ('Smash Capitalism!', 'Fight the Power!', …)

MONEY AND MOVEMENT

One example of such a directional demand would be the demand for a guaranteed and global 'basic income' or 'social wage'. In many ways, such a demand would be timely. Similar proposals are currently being discussed across an enormously broad spectrum, from the socially conservative libertarian Charles Murray, based at the American Enterprise Institute, to Andrea Fumagali, an economist at the University of Padua often associated with the Italian Marxist tradition of (post-)*operaismo*. However, whilst Murray and Fumagali come from almost opposite ends of the political spectrum, what they share in common is a belief in the implementability of the basic income – at least on a national or regional level. Both have gone to lengths to explain how this could be done.

Understanding the call for a global basic income as a directional demand, however, means recognising its ultimately utopian character. It is a call to undo one of the most basic tenets of capitalist social relations, namely, that the ability to reproduce oneself should be conditional upon the selling of one's labour-power on the market. It is the articulation of a desire to re-appropriate social wealth.

Precisely because of the discursive space opened up by Murray, Fumagali and others who have made (a restricted version of) the demand sound reasonable, there is an implicit flirtation with *realpolitik* here. Most likely it is this very fact that presents the demand with its greatest chance of being taken up by a broad movement, whether that be around (un)employment reforms, against lay-offs or by 'really existing' social movements around the issue of 'precariousness'. At a time when the Keynesian promise of full employment (or at least the safety net of the welfare state) is long dead, and when the theory and practice of neoliberalism are entering a deep

crisis, the generalisation and taking hold of such a demand could have tremendously far-reaching consequences.

Further examples of directional demands could focus on migration, its movements and struggles: 'For the Right to Remain', 'For the Right to Legalisation', 'Close All Detention Centres', or even 'For the Right to (Equal) Rights'.

To many with a background in radical social movements, these demands may seem limited. Some might understand them as little more than a humanitarian plea for sympathy with those fleeing oppression or seeking a better life, leaving the causes of flight unchallenged. Others may interpret the recourse to a 'rights' discourse in particular as a tacit acknowledgement of state/sovereign power, thereby reinforcing that power. This hugely underestimates the radical essence of these demands.

Despite ongoing processes of globalisation and what Hardt and Negri in their book *Empire* have called the scrambling of worlds, 'so that we continually find the First World in the Third, the Third in the First, and the Second almost nowhere at all', the world remains stratified. Empire, as a completely 'smooth space', has yet to be fully realised. The global political economy remains organised in such as way that it depends upon labour-power sold in different parts of the world being differently remunerated. Migration and other forms of resistance to border control and illegalisation undermine this stratification which is one of the primary bases upon which capital accumulation is organised on a world scale today.

Migration currently constitutes the world's largest social movement. It is a form of antagonism in itself. Over the last few years, however, it has taken a more overt, obviously political form. In October 2005, for example, coordinated groups of 200–500 migrants stormed the border fences of the Spanish enclaves of Ceuta and Melilla. Spanish and Moroccan border guards opened fire and mass deportations commenced. In March the following year, over a million migrant workers took to the streets of the US, protesting against the Border Protection, Anti-Terrorism and Illegal Immigration Control Act, demanding legalisation. In France, in November 2005, the *banlieue* erupted after two teenagers (a 15 and 17 year old whose parents came from Mali and Tunisia respectively) died from electrocution whilst attempting to evade a police ID control on the border of the Parisian suburb Clichy-sous-Bois. Most recently, in November 2006, detainees at Harmondsworth 'removal centre' on the outskirts of London rebelled to try and prevent their deportation.

The articulation of demands such as the right to legalisation necessarily implies a recognition that the global border regime is resisted, as well as lending this resistance political and practical support. At their base, such demands articulate our common desire to re-appropriate control over space from capital; for all of us to become the cartographers of another possible world.

TRANSITIONS AND DIRECTIONS

The idea of building a coalition, movement, party or 'class power' on the basis of a set of demands is of course, in itself, nothing new. The late-19th and early-20th century, for example, saw social democratic movements develop the concept of 'minimum' and 'maximum' demands. Some, such as Kautsky and the German Social Democratic Party, saw the minimum programme as a means of improving the conditions of workers' lives, until the inevitable collapse of capitalism. Others saw it as the most appropriate means of building a mass party capable of then moving on to a maximum programme of demands, aimed more directly towards the creation of the conditions for socialism. The social democrats, however, were widely criticised – by the Third and then the Fourth Internationals, amongst others – for consistently failing to move beyond their minimum programme. Famously, in *The Death Agony of Capitalism*, Trotsky set out an alternative series of 'transitional demands', taken up at the Fourth International's founding conference.

It would be well worth asking, then, how (or if!) directional demands are any different. What is it about them that offers more potential than these previous strategies? Indeed, are directional demands anything more than old ideas in new packaging? Seeing as, at first glance, there would appear to be a number of similarities (and indeed, there probably are) between transitional and directional demands, it is worth proposing a number of theses as to where they differ.

I. The realisation of directional demands (either individually, or when combined) would necessitate a break with capitalist social relations. Whereas transitional demands (nationalisation, employment for all, decent living conditions), like the minimum programme of classical social democracy, may be realisable within bour-

WHAT WOULD IT MEAN TO WIN?

geois society, the demand, for example, for a basic income looks for a way out. As such, the demand needs to be for its global implementation, for it to be unconditional (e.g. not dependent upon legal status), and to be sufficient to ensure that income becomes permanently de-linked from productivity.

II. Directional demands do not privilege any area of the multitude over another. Whereas Trotsky's transitional demands (along with much of the rest of 'orthodox' Marxism) have placed primacy upon the role of the industrial proletariat as political vanguard, under conditions of post-Fordism where production has spilled out of the factory and into society at large, the project for the self-constitution of an anti-capitalist social subject must do the same. Efforts towards class recomposition today must base themselves on the constitution of the common amongst the irreducible multiplicity of productive singularities through a constant process of becoming.

III. Directional demands can only be determined and decided upon by the movements themselves. Whilst transitional demands were both articulated by, and had as their goal the strengthening of, the Party, directional demands are those that emerge from, and are taken up by, the movement of antagonistic subjectivities. In this sense, there is no limit upon the number of demands which can be articulated, nor upon those who can articulate them, nor the form that this articulation can take.

IV. Directional demands constitute what Deleuze might call 'a line of flight'. Transitional demands aim towards the sweeping away of 'bourgeois rule', with a clear – and closed – idea of what should come next; namely, 'the conquest of power by the proletariat' (Trotsky). Directional demands, in contrast, seek to open up unlimited and undetermined possibilities for another world. The teleology of Hegelian and

This article draws upon discussions which have been taking place within the radical Left in Germany, and in particular the theory and practice being developed by FelS (www.fels-berlin.de) and the Interventionist Left. For those wishing to read in more detail into the debate about directional demands, see in particular Rätz and Seibert's chapter in *Losarbeiten – Arbeitslos?* (Unrast Press, 2005) and a number of articles published in issue 34 of *arranca!* magazine. Trotsky's primary text on the notion of 'transitional demands' is *The Death Agony of Capitalism and the Tasks of the Fourth International*, and the classic text detailing the social democratic strategy of the minimum and maximum programme is the so-called *Erfurt Program*, written by Karl Kautsky in 1891. Both are available online. The concepts of 'lines of flight', 'de-territorialisation' and 'plane of immanence' come from Deleuze. See in particular, 'Many Politics' in *Dialogues II* (published by Continuum). I would like to thank the Notes from Nowhere collective (www.weareeverywhere.org) for an insightful and inspiring exchange of emails on this and many other topics.

Leninist Marxisms is rejected. There is neither a predetermined destination, nor any necessary stages through which we have to pass. Directional demands seek to bring about a deterritorialisation, an opening up onto a 'plane of immanence'. As the name implies, they suggest a direction; nothing more, nothing less.

Directional demands, then, aim to provide a point around which a potential movement could consolidate. Their realisation would necessitate not only a break with the present state of things, but open up the potential for (rather than have already closed down) possible future worlds. The articulation of such demands is the monopoly of no single social actor, but rather constitutes an expression of the material struggles of the multitude of productive singularities within a process of recomposition. And finally, it is not only key in which direction such demands point, but also where they come from. As with the condition for participation in the Zapatista's *Otra Campaña* (Other Campaign) this can only be from below and – like the heart – to the left.

Ben Trott is an editor of *Turbulence.*

very different from and even skeptical of, unions. Secondly, because it shows that the companies we're fighting against are everywhere in the world and that the only way to stand up to them is by going global as well. It is only then that we will 'win'.

RN It's important to explain what these companies are, and how the cleaning industry is organised. At the top you have the owners of the office buildings, which are banks and investors like HSBC and Merril Lynch. These can be found in any financial centre of the world. Below them you have the building management companies who take care of the daily running of the buildings. Many of these are also global. Finally, you have the cleaning companies, many of which are also global. So when workers get organised, they are fighting against the cleaning companies directly, but the money comes from the top – corporations with a much higher public profile, which want to be known for their investment in the arts or their charity work, not for making a profit by squeezing the wages of those who keep their offices clean. So these companies are the ones who actually have the power to force cleaning companies to raise the standards of the industry.

VA That's it. And it's all about building leverage against them. If a company has a thousand people working for them in a city, it's pointless to organise fifty workers. You have to have the majority of the overall number of cleaners involved to make the companies, and the workers themselves, believe that a change is inevitably going to happen, standards are going to be raised. But of course, a victory against ISS in Houston doesn't change the conditions of ISS workers in London. So you have to organise there as well. Now imagine if we get to the point where there are campaigns like Justice for Janitors (J4J) in all the big centres of the world acting in coordination to force a change in the whole industry. Not just cleaners, but all workers in building services. This is what the global project of the SEIU is about: it's 'Justice for Janitors goes global'. That is, moving from defensive to offensive struggles. Trade unions are big institutions with lots of resources and political weight, but there are very few seriously organising on the ground. It's painful to see so many unions complaining about the loss of rights and the precaritisation of labour relations, seeing years of workers' achievements rolled back without figuring out how to fight back.

This is because organising at the ground level stopped a long time ago. We make a distinction between the 'organising' model of J4J and the traditional 'service' model. In the latter, the workers sign up for legal protection, advice, etc. but the relation is individualised: I'm a worker, I have a problem, I call up the union who comes and solves the problem for me. In the organising model, you have people from the union on the ground to help workers get organised. So when there's a problem, it's not 'the union' who comes around and solves it. The organiser is there to help people organise around the problem – pass a petition, organise a meeting with colleagues, produce leaflets – so instead of getting solved by a third party, what you get is a change in the balance of power in the workplace. The managers will know better next time: they'll see these workers can stand up for themselves. At the same time, it's not a matter of just getting a small victory, such as getting someone reinstated – although that's very important to build up confidence and send the bosses a message. But what you really want is people active in a larger campaign to change the industry; and of course, in order to change the industry, they'll have to change the balance of power in their workplaces, and help export their experience there to other buildings, to workers in other companies. This is why we can afford to be on the offensive, while other unions are losing members: our goal is to build organisation, capacity to act, rather than have lots of card-carrying members who only turn up when they have a problem.

RN You spoke of leverage, measuring the balance of forces and knowing what you need to produce change. A huge part of the J4J model is about research.

VA Research is the first step, before the organising begins. First, you need to identify a 'universe'. What is the size of the market? Who are the players involved (owners, building management, cleaning companies)? What share of the market do they have? How many cleaners work for each one? How many cleaners are there in total? This will give you an idea of where to build strength. It would be pointless to have all the workers in one company join the campaign, and none everywhere else, if that company only has a tiny fraction of the overall market. This particular company could decide to pay more, which is good, but in the long term it will lose all contracts to cheaper companies and thus the workers will lose their jobs to other exploited workers. This is why density matters. This is what being on the offensive is also about: identifying targets, and how to affect them; and then having the means to move in.

RN Then you start mapping this universe onto the territory: which are the buildings with the highest density of workers? Who owns them, and what companies clean them? But also: what are the conditions and pay in this and that company?– bearing in mind that even within a single company this can vary a lot.

VA Yes. So after a good deal of the research is done, the organisers move in. Hang out in front of the buildings to identify when shifts change, and try to speak to workers as they go in or out. Get more information about the workplace (how many people? how much do they make? where are most of the people from?), and start a conversation just by questioning the conditions they work in. They listen, talk about the reason for those conditions (lack of power), discuss possible solutions – this we call 'agitation'. And then we pose the question, or they pose it themselves: what can we do about it? That's when you tell them about the union, explain what the campaign is about, and show them that it's not some pie-in-the-sky utopia, but something that has been done before and can be done again. Make them think about how the industry is organised, where the leverage is, who you need to put pressure on, and how the workers from different buildings can make it happen. If they're up for it, you get their phone number and call them up again a few days later to arrange another meeting, see if they can bring some colleagues. If they do, you know they're committed, and that's where the organising begins.

After gaining critical mass in some key sites, you have organising committee meetings, which is where the organic leaders and activists from different places come together. For almost everyone it's the first time they meet each other, and it's very empowering to see other people who are in the same position, and that you probably wouldn't have met otherwise. It creates the feeling that *Sí, se puede!* ['Yes, we can!', slogan of J4J in the US, where the majority of members are Hispano-American]. At these meetings, people discuss and exchange information, including tips on how to talk to their colleagues, and plan next steps. It's both a space for education and for strategy.

RN Even at this moment, the research element is still present – it only moves from the union researchers to the organisers and workers. A huge part of the organising work is mapping the social networks inside and around the workplace: finding out how many people there are in the workplace, where they are from, what languages they speak, how they feel about the campaign. Inside, you start working out who's close to whom, who might be closer to management than to the other workers, who are the people that everyone respects, who are the people who are committed, who is indifferent, who is against the campaign. You keep charts and notebooks that are constantly updated, first by the organiser, then by the workplace leaders themselves.

VA Lots of people don't like it when we speak of 'leaders' – they think we go around appointing our favourites. If it were that, there would be no future. It's by mapping these social networks, as you said, that you identify organic leaders. We don't appoint them, the other workers do.

RN They're the point where these networks overlap, the most connected nodes.

VA And they can be for or against the union, or indifferent. If they're against it, you need to try to make them neutral. And you need to find other people in that workplace who'll be able to get everyone active.

This, like everything else in a campaign, is done incrementally. Has this person come to organising committee meetings? Then they're obviously committed. Did they bring people with them? Then they're capable of moving the others. It's the same thing with actions: you start with something small, leafleting or a picket with the members of the organising committee. As the committee grows, you start planning bigger actions, and stressing to them that it's their responsibility to make it grow, to get others active.

When the campaign kicks off, you must have a body of members ready for taking action, but you must keep an eye on many other variables. You need to find political support outside, among politicians too, but mostly the workers' communities, religious groups etc. You must develop reliable media contacts, as well as prepare leaders to deal with the press. You must keep an eye on the agenda, because timing is crucial – like knowing how to exploit it when banks announce their annual bonuses, or taking advantage of symbolic dates. All these variables run in parallel lines, and you need to coordinate them in order to create a build-up, and get to the point where these companies are getting phone calls from members of the public, being criticised in the newspapers, having religious leaders turn up on their doorstep...

RN Or having their offices in several different countries visited on the same day...

VA Until it becomes unsustainable for them. Then when one of them folds, the whole industry in that city follows. Eventually all companies sign an agreement with the union. After that, the campaign is over and what we call 'internal organising' begins: absorbing the new members into the union, creating strong representative structures in every workplace – and hopefully, from the people who became involved in that campaign, some will become future leaders of the union.

RN You mentioned the communities; a lot of the mapping is about identifying which are the areas where large numbers of the workers live, which are the churches they go to, how their national or ethnic community is organised, what are the media of communication (newspapers, radios) the community has... Activating these transversal lines can produce support for the campaign, but can sometimes produce a lot more. In London the Justice for Cleaners campaign had a clear impact in groups working around migration; it created new possibilities, providing access to infrastructure, opening channels of communication between people inside and outside institutions. It's still too early to say if it will have the same impact as J4J in the US, but one can see the differences – also in the fact that the union [Transport and General Workers' Union, host of Justice for Cleaners] has become a lot more assertive in its defence of migrants, and taken a public position in favour of regularisation.

VA It depends on the context, too; in the US, very often we have members who already have a memory of struggle in their countries of origin. I worked with former Sandinistas, for example! Also black and Hispanic churches in the US have a long history of involvement in civil rights struggles, and are important nodes of political organisation in the community.

RN This is the most important element of J4J, I'd say. A campaign in itself could be described as business unionism, but it is part and parcel of the J4J model that you activate the community, you create new, transversal connections – which is what you could call social unionism. For me that's the most important element: at the end of the day, with J4J as with anything else, there's no guarantee that relations won't become crystallised, that you won't just create a new representative class. But if a campaign successfully feeds into a lively movement around it – a movement that can also, to some extent, reclaim the union as its own – then you have more chances of there always being enough pressure 'from below' to keep things moving.

VA Not just that; the movement can do things that the union can't. The union is limited in various ways by legal or structural constraints. So if something needs to be done that the union can't do, it's important to have the support of those who can. Almost all our members are migrants, often with an irregular status. They can't do a sit-in and risk being arrested, but others can. If there are housing problems in a place, it's not our direct job to start a campaign, but we can support those who do. At the same time, it's important that these relations are very clear and open. I helped organise J4J marches supported by the Black Bloc, and they knew there could be no trouble because of people's legal status – so you had all these kids in black marching alongside Mexican grandmothers, pacifists, American Indian Movement members, university and high school students, migrant rights organisations.

Also, what you say about reclaiming the union... A union victory has the effect of spreading this feeling of possibility to everyone else. This was certainly one of the things that led to such a vibrant migrant movement in the US in the last few years – people saw their friends and family organise and win, and started organising too. J4J has had an important role in the struggle for migrant legalisation in the US. A direct role, by participating in coordinations, co-organising marches, building alliances.

RN You mentioned legal constraints. I think this is one area where the approximation with something like J4J also highlights something important. For example, many 'activists' of the 'autonomous' kind criticise unions for accepting given legislation; but that also shows that autonomy is always to a certain extent staked against the State, and on that level legislation does count a lot. A friend and I were talking about it: there's recently been highly publicised cases of local governments moving to evict squatted social centres that have lasted for decades (Umdogshuset in Copenhagen, Les Tanneries in Dijon, Köpi in Berlin). When this happens, people go there from all over Europe to try and defend what they already have. But wouldn't an offensive way of doing it be to collect the most progressive bits of squatting legislation in different countries, and start campaigning for a progressive European legislation on the subject, while keeping on squatting at the same time? It's similar to what the MST (Landless Peasants Movement) is doing in Brazil: if the legal definition of 'productive' land is changed, there will be a lot more land that can be rightfully occupied.

VA It's always best to take the initiative, particularly in areas like European legislation that are still to be invented, and in the hands of bureaucrats. Every territory is important in the struggle; the legal territory is crucial. If we get back to the point where unions can mobilise people, we can revert the negative legislation passed when unions were impotent; this will mean we can do more, go further. It's like a campaign, you go step-by-step. Our rights to organise are under attack in the US and everywhere, and this is one of the biggest fights for the next few years. Everyone assumes we have the right to organise in our workplaces, but the reality is very different. You might have the right but no power to enforce it. In the US existing rights are minimal. So you need a two-pronged strategy: you need a strong movement, and that strong movement needs to sustain people who will fight on the level of legislation and institutions.

RN Perhaps this is where one distinction between 'radicals' and 'reformists' could be drawn: 'reformists' will always work under the given legal constraints; 'radicals' will take them as limits for the struggle at this moment but work to build up the struggle so that those limits can be overturned.

VA What people who see unions as reformist should do is work with them, from the inside and the outside, to push them towards being more radical.

Valery Alzaga has worked for the Service Employees' International Union (SEIU) as a labour organiser in the Justice for Janitors (J4J) campaign for over nine years, but she defines herself first of all as a 'global justice' activist; she has been in Europe for two years, working for the SEIU global department, having collaborated in the setting up of campaigns in London, Hamburg and the Hague. Rodrigo Nunes, also on the editorial collective of *Turbulence*, worked in the Justice for Cleaners campaign in London from 2005 to 2006. He worked as a community organiser and popular educator in Brazil, and now lives in London, where he is finishing a PhD in philosophy with a grant from CAPES – Brazilian Government. More info on J4J at http://www.seiu.org/property/janitors/

Solidarity economics

Euclides André Mance

A DARING HYPOTHESIS: there is a global revolution underway. It is not led by any political party or vanguard. It has no military bases and its strategy is anti-belligerent. It mobilises millions of people all over the world. We know little about it. What we do know is that at the grassroots level of its mobilisations, organisation and popular education, there are thousands of movements and millions of people who have begun weaving collaborative networks of economic solidarity, creating channels and connections with the potential to bring together and strengthen local and global struggles. They are working collectively, from the bottom up, and democratically, building consensus while respecting reasoned dissent. We see these movements and their achievements everywhere, yet we know little about the power of this phenomenon, for at first they seem insufficient in number and size to change the world. And yet, I maintain: there is a global revolution underway.

The great political discovery of the 1990s was the idea of weaving collaborative networks among groups, movements and organisations through which to coordinate and share, not only our solutions and victories, but also our problems and challenges, our strategies and everyday practices. We were creating axes of struggle capable of bringing together the local and the global, the long and short term, as well as diversity and unity. However, while these collaborative networks were crucial, we had not understood their full potential.

Take the example of the World Social Forums; the WSF process is the tip of a giant iceberg hiding myriad collaborative networks and processes. The limit of the WSF process is that it has not gone nearly far enough in developing world social networks. The forums are important moments connecting thousands of actors, opening up a significant flow of communication of the diversities that are inherent to these networks. Afterwards, even if participants are somehow informed by the new, collectively acquired experience, the flows of communication and actions essentially return to the previously existing plateaus.

While clearly important, processes and spaces such as social forums are not enough. Taking the global construction of collaborative solidarity networks as our strategic horizon means finding ways of promoting, reinforcing and expanding on such moments in more spheres of life and struggle. More than simply spreading information about proposals, and thus acting on the level of ideological debate, it is necessary to operate on political and economic planes, putting some of the proposals into practice. In other words, our daily economic practices must be part of the work of transforming global economic structures.

Beyond social forums and summit mobilisations, the defence of sovereign economies must happen in the choice of products we consume, and the ethical decision to employ our income to strengthen certain economic sectors rather than others. The same applies to our defence of ecosystems, and the choice to reduce the environmental impact of our consumption. The 'good fight' must be fought on the economic plane (not just in culture or politics). There is a revolution underway, but 'to be winning' means expanding and strengthening the collaborative processes that may form the base from which a possible post-capitalist society can emerge.

SOLIDARITY ECONOMY AS THE MATERIAL BASE OF POST-CAPITALIST SOCIETIES

Millions of people across the world practise solidarity economy. They work and consume in order to produce for their own and other people's welfare, rather than for profit. In solidarity economy what matters is creating satisfactory economic conditions for all people. This means assuring individual and collective freedoms, generating work and income, abolishing all forms of exploitation, domination and exclusion, and protecting ecosystems as well as promoting sustainable development.

This network initially came out of successful practices of work and income generation, fair trade, ethical consumption, solidarity finance, and the diffusion of sustainable productive technologies. These efforts were, however, isolated. It was necessary for them to develop into collaborative networks that integrated these diverse actions with strategies that increased the potential of economic flows and the interconnections between them. This meant that solidarity finance could enable the emergence and maintenance of worker-managed productive enterprises that employed low-impact technologies and promoted the highest social benefit. The products of these enterprises started being commercialised in circuits of solidarity trade through shops, fairs, international fair trade systems and even internet sales. This in turn enabled consumers to replace the products and services they bought from capitalist enterprises with products and services produced within the solidarity economy, feeding back into a system of promotion of welfare for workers and

'The term 'solidarity economy' is the English translation of *economia solidária* (Portuguese), *economía solidaria* (Spanish), and *économie solidaire* (French). Broadly defined, it names a grassroots form of cooperative economics that is working throughout the world to connect thousands of local alternatives together to create large-scale, viable, and creative networks of resistance to the profit-over-all-else economy...

Like all terms of political struggle, the definition of 'solidarity economy' is widely contested. For some, it refers to a set of strategies aimed at the abolition of capitalism and the oppressive social relations that it supports and encourages; for others, it names strategies for 'humanising' the capitalist economy – seeking to supplement capitalist globalisation with community-based 'social safety nets'.' – *Ethan Miller*

'Tenant organisations, unemployed associations, cooperative nurseries, consumer clubs, solidarity credit associations, local currencies, and more: all these activities share a common characteristic of willfully going against the predominant economic model; they emphasise local solutions before anything else; they bond economic construction with its environment. They are new, freely chosen and democratically arbitrated forms of redistribution that are focused on the needs of men and women.' – *Inter-Reseaux de l'Economie Solidaire, France*
from: http://www.geo.coop/SolidarityEconomicsEthanMiller.htm

consumers, environmental protection and sustainable development. Technologies such as free software and organic agriculture began being employed, developed and shared across these networks. Excess wealth produced in the circuit was reinvested, part of it in the form of solidarity microfinance.

However fast solidarity economy is developing, millions of people who fight for 'another world' do not practise or participate in it. First, because they are unaware of it; second, because of the relatively difficult access to the products and services produced within this other economy. Both difficulties can be quickly surmounted. The main obstacle is cultural: to overcome a consumerist culture that prizes quantity, excess, possession and waste over the welfare of people and communities, we need to replace unsustainable forms of production, consumption and ways-of-life with the affirmation of new ways of producing, consuming and living in solidarity.

As they progress in the economic and cultural terrains of this revolution, solidarity networks will also advance in the political sphere – transforming the State, creating and reinforcing mechanisms of popular participation. There is no linearity in this revolution; each reality changes in its own way. But by virtue of their being-in-network, collaborative processes can communicate and learn from each historical experience, successful or not. The information technologies that facilitate their interconnection tend to become increasingly central to the State and the public sphere. This opens up the possibility of new processes and mechanisms of governance and shared management that can result from the combined effects of democratic revolutions in the cultural sphere with collaborative solidarity economic processes as its material base.

CHALLENGES AND HORIZONS
Of course, all is not that simple, and huge challenges and questions, both practical and theoretical, remain. For starters some key questions that are often posed:
- In what way do solidarity economy networks relate to their outside, the capitalist economy? Are these external relations based on competition? If that is the case, how can solidarity economy 'win'?
- How can we make sure that the expansion of solidarity economy networks would not mean a loss of its initial principles? In general, in what ways can the networks themselves enforce their principles? And is the creation of jobs and incomes not more important than these 'principles'?
- What distinguishes the defence of solidarity economy from a defence of localist forms of capitalism? Does it amount to more than a mere commitment to local welfare, and to what extent is that commitment not compatible with a local, 'small-scale' capitalism?
- How does solidarity economy move in the horizon of contemporary Latin American politics?

The more the solidarity economy expands and diversifies, and its flows and connections improve, the smaller the need to relate to non-solidarity actors. The underlying logic is to progressively reduce relations with non-solidarity providers and distributors, putting in their place relations with solidarity actors who then become integrated with the networks. While relating to non-solidarity actors, solidarity economy initiatives strive to select the socially and ecologically 'least bad' providers and distributors.

While some fear that an expansion of collaborative networks and solidarity economy would quickly replicate the competition-based mechanisms of non-solidarity economy, I believe it is the best strategy to ensure the 'victory' of solidarity economy initiatives over the rest. For the expansion itself affirms confidence in another economy, based on collaboration and not competition As such, the focus should not be on developing strategies to push non-solidarity initiatives out of the market, but to multiply the number and diversity of solidarity actors to such an extent that it would enable a reorganisation of productive chains along which an environmentally sustainable and socially just economy could develop.

Thus, solidarity economy should not be confused with the capitalist mode of production. Some people mistake it for 'local development'; and since capitalism

SOLIDARITY ECONOMIES – A BACKGROUND
by Turbulence

Social currency is an alternative currency issued by communities or networks. It replaces State-issued currency, sometimes in situations where the latter is not available, creating a medium for exchanges in an economy that take place 'outside' the official one. Social currencies can be of two kinds: guaranteed and non-guaranteed against reserves.

There are many different ways in which networks can deal with *interest rates*. For example, by stipulating a fixed amount of credit that any individual can have at all times; this stops inflation, but keeps the volume of the economy always at the same level. Some experiences have been made with negative interest rates. In this case, currency is considered a common good which is put to its proper use when generating trade. Therefore, anyone who accumulates credit without putting it in circulation is taxed X amount at a given period. This stimulates trade and limits the amount of currency available. Not only does this represent a way of controlling inflation without interest rates, it also moves power from the hand of creditors to the hands of producers.

When the Grameen Bank in Bangladesh started providing small loans to people below the poverty line, two hypotheses were proved: that those taking the loans most of the time would pay them back in time; and that normally all it took was a little push to get small productive initiatives off the ground. *Micro-credit* is a form of strengthening the economic dynamics of a community. For instance, when a local bank provides a textile cooperative with financing for a small productive project (buying more machines, for example), this means that the cooperative will be is capable of promoting local development, they imagine solidarity economy can be reduced to that perspective of localism. Capitalist initiatives of this kind have been successful in some cases, with significant support from State actors; but with time, the logic of concentration of wealth always ends up weakening local economic dynamism.

In turn, even if it is true that solidarity economy promotes territorial development, it cannot be forgotten that the way in which it does so is under the paradigm of wealth distribution rather than capital accumulation. The more wealth is distributed, through the practice of fair prices (in the commercialisation of goods and services as well as the remuneration of self-managed work), the greater the local welfare in general. These fair prices are fixed by the economic actors themselves – enterprises, producers, consumers who relate to each other directly in each transaction – in a way that is coordinated across networks. Solidarity economy is based on a set of values at once ethical and economic, that are materialised in concrete practices such as self-management, democratic decision-making about economic activity and the ecological reorganisation of productive chains. If all the important decisions are

producing more affordable clothes for the local population, and the profit made will allow members of the cooperative to buy food from the local shop, allowing its owner to pay the rent etc. In some cases loan-takers have to provide alienable guarantees, in others not. *Solidarity guarantee*, where a small group of people pool together to provide the conditions for taking the loan, is very common. As people prove they are able to pay back in time, the size of the loans grow. Other famous examples of micro-credit banks are BancoSol, in Bolivia (today a private bank) and Palmas, in Brazil (which has existed since 1998 and is entirely community-run).

A *barter system* is an economic system that can function without any official currency. It is a system of exchanges, where participants can exchange goods and services for other goods services directly (for example, I can 'buy' food from you by 'selling' you a haircut). This type of relation always exists informally to some extent, but it can be formalised in the form of barter clubs, allowing for bigger and more complex systems. In these cases, they normally involve the use of a social currency. This facilitates trade of goods and services whose difference in value is more difficult to quantify; for example, in exchange for three months of language lessons, I can give you a pair of shoes plus *X* amount of social currency. In this case, prices can be fixed directly between individuals, or, through collective decision-making processes. In becoming a member of the club, each person receives *X* amount of credit in social currency that they must pay back if or when they leave; different clubs can become organised in larger networks that use the same currency, or accept each other's. Further reading: *http://www.zmag.org/content/showarticle.cfm?ItemID=10926*
http://www.communityeconomies.org/
http://www.socioeco.org/en/

made in assemblies, it is highly unlikely that this self-management could result in the negation of the very democracy that founds it.

Among the main risks run by solidarity economy today, two are: the little understanding that progressive social forces have of it; and the incursions capitalistic forces have been making around the notion of solidarity, attaching it to the idea of social responsibility. Many thus conclude that solidarity economy is simply a form of capitalism that takes social responsibility seriously. This prejudice, particularly within the Left, along with certain sectors of the right, turns the burden of proof against solidarity economy, forcing it to present justifications regarding its historical possibility rather than drawing the debate to the effectiveness of its present historical reality – one where workers have become owners of self-managed enterprises and decide democratically what to do with them, collaborating with other enterprises in ways that are advantageous to all. On the other hand, solidarity economy actors looking for funding from public, particularly State bodies, tone down the antagonistic and revolutionary character of this new economy, creating room for ambiguous readings that allow them to be lumped in with social and environmental responsibility talk. Moreover, while the debate rages on about whether the values of solidarity economy will not get lost along the way, large chunks of progressive social sectors still consume non-solidarity products without questioning the effects of their consumption, which feeds back into local and global capitalist circuits.

Nonetheless, in Latin America, solidarity economy is advancing quickly, learning from both its mistakes and achievements. In Argentina, for example, after an initial explosion in the number of barter groups with their own local currencies – which at one point reached over two million participants and some surveys suggest three to five million – these networks quickly declined in size again. The seriousness of the impasse led to the emergence of a new national network of solidarity barter, with improved organisation and methodology. In Brazil the lessons from Argentina and other places led to the creation of community banks that operate through social currencies locally issued and circulated, which are, as opposed to the Argentinian case pre-impasse, guaranteed against reserves with solidarity micro-credit funds. In Venezuela, the Brazilian experience has inspired the ongoing organisation of a network of community banks that issue local currencies. In Mexico, a system of exchange has been developed where social currencies are no longer issued on paper, but registered as electronic credit on smart cards that allow for the transactions to take place through networks of data communication. In Brazil, the electronic system developed enables the realisation of transactions both with non-guaranteed currencies, which circulate only within a group of users-issuers, and guaranteed ones, as a form of payment between any users of the system, without the need for smart cards.

We can thus see that these experiences, both through their successes and their failures, have been a valuable source of knowledge: thanks to the flows of communication among collaborative networks, solidarity economy in Latin America has been capable of growing.

CONCLUSION

In Brazil 1.2 million workers are, integrally or partially, involved in solidarity economy and 1,250 enterprises have appeared in the last five years. This may not seem much, but this is a phenomenon that has grown over the last decade – reflected in a growing awareness of participants themselves, as shown by the proliferation of solidarity economy forums all over Brazil and the world, and the parallel intensification of transactions within the sector and the advance in its political expression.

If for many it is only a utopia, an ever-receding horizon of hope, for millions of others solidarity economy is a way of working, producing, commercialising, consuming and exchanging values. It is a way of satisfying individual and personal needs in the interest of the welfare of all. It is the material base of the network revolution.

Solidarity economy is the base of a new mode of production that propagates itself through the network revolution. In this sense, 'we are winning', because solidarity economy is in expansion, networks proliferate everywhere and their capacity for political action increases – one can see this in the wave of popular governments that have been victorious in elections all over Latin America. But this revolution depends on our ability to keep connecting and expanding into 'networks of networks', 'movements of movements', bringing local and global together. Our everyday practices must be guided by principles of solidarity, and our choices must be in agreement with the world we want to build. For that, we must strengthen the circuits of solidarity economy.

Translated from Portuguese by Rodrigo Nunes

Euclides André Mance is a philosopher and has been a popular educator since the 1990s. He is a member of the Popular Solidarity Economy Network in Brazil, and animator of the website www.solidarius.com.br. He is the author of various texts and books, such as *The Network Revolution* [*A Revolução das redes*], which has been translated into Italian. His work can be found on http://www.milenio.com.br/mance/

Compositional power

An interview with Todd Hamilton and Nate Holdren, members of the Industrial Workers of the World (IWW)

Why prioritise workplace organisation when some people have argued value production now takes place everywhere?

We work for wages. We spend a huge chunk of our day and our lives at work, so it just makes sense for us to organise there. We don't see this as a choice for people who want a revolution: we have to be organising in the workplace now, so that when opportunities open up we're already there. Whether the revolution begins amongst housewives, chronically unemployed, housing struggles, etc., we're still going to need to deal with workplaces in the transformation of society.

As far as value production now taking place everywhere... well this isn't actually a new condition, it's always been true wherever capitalism has existed. Your question implies that since value production occurs everywhere, there's no need to organise in the workplace. We see it instead as meaning we need to organise in many places.

So has nothing changed? What about increasing precarity, for example?

No. A lot has changed. But since life outside of waged workplaces has always been part of value production, we don't see this as one major change which changes everything else (which is what some people seem to think with real subsumption, post-Fordism, postmodernity, whatever). This whole debate has produced some important insights into the way we understand the capitalist mode of production,

exploitation, hierarchy, and so on. But many people mistake the innovation in theory for a change in the material conditions of the present. This is unfortunate for two reasons. First, we think these new theories can help us better understand the past too. And, second, there are important lessons from past experiences which we need to hang onto as a tool for use in the present. If everything has changed, as some argue, then the status of those lessons/examples is lessened.

There have been changes though. One big change in the US is that the ruling class is largely no longer interested in the class compromise upon which the higher unionisation rates in the US were once built – the business unions negotiated higher productivity in exchange for better conditions. The ruling class has decided it can accomplish much of what it wants without having to cut any such deal, by simply forcing higher productivity and worse pay and conditions. But this isn't a change at the level of production, it's a change in demeanor of the ruling class, how old laws are interpreted, new laws being invented, etc. Simultaneously the makeup of the US workforce has shifted – more immigrant labour in certain sectors, more service-industry work where conditions breed high turnover.

For an interesting take on biopolitical syndicalism from an Argentinian perspective, see Franco Ingrassia's article, available in English at http://whatinthehell.blogsome.com/2006/07/27/is-biopolitical-sindicalism/

So what are the problems of workplace organising? And if material conditions haven't changed substantially, why is the IWW a fraction of the size and strength it was 90 years ago?

The main problems for the IWW, and worker organising in general, are not a result of epochal shifts in capitalism. Take precarity, which you mention. We just don't think there's been a significant change here: precarity is the universal condition of the proletariat. Perhaps this condition was obscured for many years for large sections of the working class – the basis of the post-war settlement – but the people the IWW organised most and most successfully were outside these sections. Labour conditions in some of the sectors the IWW organised historically in the US are no more precarious today than in 1912, and in some cases they are significantly less so. And, more generally, precarity was never lessened or obscured in the US to the degree that it was in some other places. That's part of the the reason why the debates on precarity in Europe haven't jumped the ocean. European precaritisation is in many ways socio-economic Americanisation.

There's a number of reasons for the IWW's decline, partly related to shifts in the economy and demographics of the US, and partly to repression. The IWW was almost destroyed several times over the course of its history. Tons and tons of organisers got murdered, permanently disabled, imprisoned, deported, blacklisted, etc. There's a parallel here with the movement(s) in Italy in the 1970s and the destruction of *autonomia*.

But workplace struggles never went away. The problem is simply that organising is really, really hard: the ruling class has the deck stacked dramatically in its favor, and even though our power is superior, making this latent power active is an arduous, dangerous, and difficult process. This is the main difficulty we face and it's pretty much true for any class struggle in any society.

In some ways increased flexibility and mobility in and out of work do make organising harder. But not impossible, and, in fact, the IWW has been the only union organising in many 'flexible' workplaces (independently contracted computer workers, transportation workers, etc.). But despite these changes in the composition of the class, our model of organisation doesn't vary much.

What is solidarity unionism and how does it relate to other models of workplace organisation, like bio-syndicalism or Justice for Janitors?

Talk of a solidarity unionism 'model' is a bit misleading. It's more like a scale or a key in music, it provides the framework within which we improvise the affective, immaterial, flexible processes of organising and building organisation. Simply put solidarity unionism is organising collectively to directly implement our desires, whether that's in a single workplace, across an industry, or throughout the whole economy. It's an attempt to construct or exercise collective power against an employer (or the employing class), with the intention of making them do something they would not otherwise do. It's about organising whether we're recognised or not, whether there's a contract or not, and most of all settling direct worker issues by the workers directly. Our goal is the (prefigurative) transformation of social relations within the workplace, while building experience of struggle and class consciousness amongst its participants.

A solidarity union is a shared project. Grammatically speaking, it exists in the first person plural. Considered from outside this first person perspective, the union is something else, just as I am only I when considered from the first person perspective. Furthermore, it is best to think about solidarity unions in terms of subjective rather than objective pronouns, as I or we, not me or us. As objects, we are acted upon: the boss fired me; the union won us a 5% raise. But as subjects we act: I come to the organising meeting, we refuse to work, we collaborate together.

From the little we've learnt from comrades in Spain and Argentina, bio-syndicalism looks sort of like our kind of unionism, except it involves more of a relationship with the state than we see as necessary: demands for new rights or law, or running for election, say. Within the IWW we may have tactical relations with the state for defensive purposes, but we don't think there are any positive gains to be won this way. As workers our relationship with the boss is one of power. We cannot rely on recognition, representation or visibility to change that relationship; we can only rely on our collective organisation!

Bio-syndicalism doesn't strike us as a new idea. It's very much like some forms of organising that existed in the 1930s and before, and have continued to exist in small pockets here and there. Why call that 'bio-syndicalism' instead of just syndicalism? Our impression is that the people who like bio-syndicalism hold to a type of marxism that believes everything is different under the sun today, so that old organisational forms don't work anymore. Sure, some older organisational forms have lost their efficacy and some, like the Party and business unions, never worked in the first place. But others do still work.

And Justice for Janitors...?
While anything that makes for better conditions for workers is great, we're not particularly excited about Justice For Janitors. Justice For Janitors is part of the Service Employees International Union (SEIU), a business union in the US (part of a coalition with the overstated name 'Change To Win' which split from the AFL-CIO). Our criticisms of business unionism are many, and we see Justice For Janitors and other similar campaigns (they're called 'corporate campaigns' in the US) as repeating all these problems. In short, they all boil down to discouraging workers' self-activity and bureaucratising and defusing struggle. The business union model involves delegating power away from workers to professionals outside the workplace – paid staff and officials, lawyers, public relations people, journalists, etc. The effects on democracy in the workplace are obvious. And business unions usually aim at contracts. But once in force these become a mechanism for policing the shop floor because of the need to keep production flowing and to avoid an Unfair Labor

Practice charge against the official union (contracts all contain 'no strike' clauses, making work stoppages illegal).

What then is the difference between 'activism' and organising?

This is a crucial distinction for us. We see activism as acting for someone else: show up to a protest on someone else's behalf. Organising is acting with someone else: get together with someone else, form a group of people, start acting collectively on shared needs. Activism has a function and is important sometimes, but organising is more important. Put it this way – in activism we exert what power we have, in solidarity with someone else. In organising we get together with others in order to increase our collective power. As a result, we have more power to exert, both in solidarity with others and, in the long run, to reduce the problems that we face.

We might explain this difference by looking at the old slogan 'be realistic, demand the impossible!' We can translate 'be realistic' into 'be reasonable'. The activist makes impossible demands, then when criticised insists 'this is reasonable!' The organiser uses a reasonable approach in order to move people into thinking – and feeling in their gut, in terms of confidence – that what they used to think was impossible is actually possible.

Being an organiser means encountering someone else where they're at, using an idiom and appealing to values as close as possible to the ones they already have. The goal is to get close to them in order to move them (and be moved ourselves perhaps). But organising in the workplace also uses capacities everyone has. It presupposes, implicit or explicitly, a universal capacity to do and be more, that the actual does not exhaust the potential. This underlines an important part of what we see as the role of an organiser. If everyone is capable of organising then the organiser is only a temporary role, and one that is not monopolisable. Indeed, anyone who occupies that role should aim at the opposite of monopoly, at collectivisation.

Given the above, how do you relate to the 'movement of movements', which sometimes seems to be built around spectacular events like summit protests? And don't some 'activists' actually organise, whilst union 'organisers' might in fact be activists?

Summit mobilisations can be awesome. Take Seattle. There were tons of great people there and exciting stuff happened. Many people did stuff that went beyond their

The May 2007 International Syndicalist Conference agreed to organise an international union of Starbucks workers linking the current local unions across Europe (UK, France), North America (US, Canada) and Australasia (New Zealand). This means taking the first practical steps towards a true international union for fast food workers, setting a model whereby they can organise internationally across the industry to fight casualisation and low pay. More details from www.starbucksunion.org

positions (and others did stuff that didn't live up to their positions). But we think there are real limits to this.

There's a difference of both site and function. The summit protest's site is at a location where there's a summit. Its functions are many and include getting a lot of people into a place together for a positive experience (inspiring, educational/transformational, meeting people, communicating, etc), and physically impeding the functioning of the summit. With workplace organising the site is double: in the workplace, as the place for action against the bosses, and outside the workplace, in homes, in meeting rooms or elsewhere. Put differently, the sites are the face-to-face encounter between two or more people (outside work), and the bigger and conflictual encounter between groups of workers and their bosses/the production process (in the workplace). But we're not claiming any monopoly: we know some of these types of sites also exist in summit protests and other activism, and that's excellent.

Few people literally live at work, but almost everyone lives at work in the sense that we have to go there for our jobs. We're not there deliberately in the same way we are at a summit protest. In other words, we're not necessarily already plugged into the movement. Take the positive encounters between protesters and residents that happen at a summit protest (like when people bring food and water to protesters, cheer them on, talk to them, etc). They're really cool but aren't the reason for the protest. By contrast these types of encounter are the whole point of workplace organising. We organise at work to meet our co-workers. Or rather, organising at work is meeting (actually many, many, many meetings…) with our co-workers. The function of workplace organising is also double. First, to produce a positive experience, preferably one which leads to members of the organisation and to people becoming organisers. This isn't always or even often fun, but it is transformational and educational, both in how we see the world and in our capacities, like learning a new dance step or learning to keep cool while speaking in front of people. The second function is to increase collective power at work and therefore to improve conditions.

But the movement of movements isn't just about summit protests, is it? And we think really the question of the IWW's relationship to the movement of movements can only be answered by talking about what it is. We're not sure exactly, but nor are we interesting in drawing lines, defining who's in and who's out. Certainly we think it's likely that the transformational effects on individuals of both summit protests (say) and workplace-organising could have results for the other, as people's lives take them across different sites. Struggles mutually reinforce one another. But we don't know that either includes the other or should, at least not 'include' in the sense of 'subsumes'.

What does organising really mean in concrete, day-to-day terms? And related to that, how do you measure success or failure?

Someone we know says this: 'Everyone wants a revolution but no one wants to wash the dishes.' Organising involves a lot of dish-washing. We have a lot of conversations with people, asking them questions, listening, responding, asking follow-up questions, listening some more. We build a relationship with them. We find out what they want to see changed at work. We get them to talk with other people at work in order to build (and then strengthen) a web of relationships.

Then we start to talk and act as a group – identifying things we want to see changed, figuring out ways to pressure the boss and ways to implement the changes we want. At the concrete day-to-day level, organising is like running a really long distance – it's not particularly complicated intellectually but it takes a lot of time and energy, and it can be really hard. It is pretty slow-moving sometimes, especially when we're used to the pace and the energy of big demonstrations.

It's easier to talk about the success question. It's usual to think of success and failure in terms of winning campaigns, achieving demands, increasing membership, etc. But many of our most active members are from campaigns that didn't achieve their goals, and few active members are from campaigns that did. Betrayals, false starts, firings, attacks, and the like seem to have gotten us some of the best people, whereas gains can sometimes lead to slow deaths and few committed members – contracts leading to passive satellite shops uninterested in organising and interaction.

Of course we organise to protect ourselves and our co-workers from layoffs and from harassment, and we organise to improve our wages and benefits. But winning is not solely a matter of better wages or conditions. It's also about radicalisation and the experience of collective organising. It's collective struggle with our co-workers which expands our experience, understanding and abilities. We have seen this occur in many cases, even without winning external measurable gains.

When we struggle we reshape our lives in ways that are deeply moving for many of us, so moving that people are willing to risk their livelihoods to be a part of it. Todd was on strike at a home for children with acute behavioral problems. Almost none of the workers planned to stick around for the end of the next contract period, but they were striking for something bigger than that. Nate worked at an NGO where people started organising against bad conditions. People began to stick around out of commitment to each other, because of the relationships that they built as part of the organising. Neither of these instances created the workplace improvements we were hoping for. Judged from an external standard, our experiences were failures (as is every working class struggle which does not abolish capitalism). This external standard is important, because it reminds us of the world we must change, but it makes it difficult to draw lessons from our experiences or identify resources we have gained.

Struggle changes us, makes us different, recomposes us. When we organise on the job something is ruptured. This happens to individuals and to organisations, whether informal, like a group of friends and co-workers, or more formal, like a union. If struggles are widespread or circulate enough, they begin to effect what can be called a recomposition of the working class. The most important effect of this is to increase 'compositional power' – the individual and collective ability to organise. Compositional power is increased or made more effective by its use, like a muscle: solidarity unionism is one way of doing this.

Some of this is analogous to feminist practices of consciousness raising. It matters less if something has been said before about women's oppression and more that this particular person or group of persons comes to be able to say it – and does say it – for themselves. An agitational conversation, one involving say the question 'what is your job like?', is less about extracting knowledge and more about a performative activity in which the person has an affective experience (becomes agitated), makes a decision (to take a small action toward changing the workplace and coming together with others), begins to develop a relationship with the conversation partner, and begins to acquire the confidence, skills, and analysis needed to successfully organise their workplace.

In the end the success of organising lies in social relationships. Organising ought to prefigure the systemic shifts in social relations that the end of capitalism entails. When we struggle together and take action, we confront things that formerly we had to face alone. A bridge can be built between people engaged together in struggle, and we can drive fissures into the isolation that is imposed on us. Organising is about reclaiming our lives and our space to realise our desires, often ones we didn't even know about. It's not always easy or pleasant, but sometimes unique beauty and joy can be born of these collective transformations.

Todd Hamilton lives in Portland, Oregon, USA, and is an unemployed health care worker. He can be contacted at logos@riseup.net. Nate Holdren lives and works in Minneapolis, Minnesota, USA. He can be contacted at nateholdren@gmail.com. For more on the IWW go to www.iww.org

"Becoming-Woman?" In theory or in practice?

Michal Osterweil

> *There are no shortcuts, and if there are they are only "table tricks".*
> *There is only experimentation as method and substance of the*
> *"becoming-movement"*
> — Global Project, www.globalmagazine.org

THEORY/PRACTICE DIVIDE?

I think a big part of why many people have been so excited about the politics ushered in by the Zapatistas, Seattle, and Social Forums – to name just a bit of what constitutes the motley 'movement of movements' many speak of – is because they embodied and posited deliberate reactions to the practical and theoretical failures of previous political approaches on the Left.

That is, leftist movements, unions and parties clearly failed to achieve or effect change based on the parameters and theories they were working by: they did not defeat capitalism or achieve equality. But these failures were not primarily due to a thwarted strategy, a forced compromise or a political loss to another side. Rather, there were fundamental problems with the modes and political visions these leftist movements were using and basing their practices on. These included: the reproduction of oppressions and micro-fascisms within supposedly progressive organisations; an inability to deal with the differences posed by contextual (historical, geographic, cultural, personal) specificities; and an inability to articulate a sustainable form of relation between movements and everyday life or society, and between movements and the 'political' (i.e. the State, or other more permanent forms of political organisation). Finally these movements failed to relate to human desires – for leisure, love, fun and so on.

In contrast, one of the most inspiring things about the 'movement of movements,' is precisely the visibility and centrality of critical and reflective practices captured perhaps most famously by the Zapatista phrase *caminar preguntando* – 'to walk while questioning'. Today, almost everywhere one looks among many of the diverse movement networks, there are various attempts to think through, investigate and experiment with different political practices, imaginaries, as well as different analyses of the systems and sites in which we are struggling. Moreover, this theoretical production strives to find language and concepts adequate to the complex, messy and unexpected elements always present in the lived realities of efforts at social change.

While movements have always produced theories to help guide their action, what I find particularly notable is what seems a common tendency, among many parts of this disparate movement, in the nature of both the content of the theories, and the ways they are produced. They seem based in an ethic of partiality, specificity and open-endedness; a willingness to be revised and reworked depending on their lived effectiveness; and a sensitivity to the fact that unexpected conflicts and consequences might arise when different subjects or circumstances come into contact with them. Of no coincidence, these mirror forms of theorising and political practice that many align with feminism.

I first heard a comparison to feminism almost five years ago when I was visiting Italy in an attempt to learn about the phenomenal movement that had brought over 300,000 people to the streets of Genoa; had made Italians some of the most active participants in myriad alter-globalisation meetings and protests outside of Italy; and had seen the emergence of local social forums – where non-representative forms of government were experimented with on a regular basis – in many Italian cities. The Bologna Social Forum (BSF) was one of the most active of these local forums and I am told that, at its height, it was not unusual for 500 people to attend, many of whom were individuals not affiliated with any party, union or militant organisation. At the first meeting of the BSF I attended, one of the leaders of the then *Disobbedienti* opened his remarks with a bold and strange statement. He declared, 'Io credo che questo movimento sía una donna' – 'I believe that this movement is a woman'. He then went on to explain that what he meant was that this movement was female because it functioned according to different logics than previous movements. It functioned according to logics of difference, dispersion and affect: no central group or singular ideology could control it, and it was propelled by an energy, from subjects and places, that far exceeded those of traditional forms of leftist organisation and practice. To him this was intimately tied to feminine/feminist notions of politics – and therefore to the figure of woman.

After his remarks the space was filled with silence, smirks, smiles and some hesitant nods of agreement. I shared the ambivalence. On the one hand I was intellectually intrigued and somewhat in agreement with his claim about the 'feminine'

or minoritarian logic of this movement, but on the other, I was a bit disturbed by the comment. Besides a visceral reaction to the very use of the term 'woman' (by a man) to describe something as dynamic and heterogeneous as the (Italian) alter-globalisation movement, it made me uncomfortable because throughout a meeting lasting well over two hours, only two or three women had actually spoken. Moreover, when they did speak, they took less time and spoke with less authority than the many male activists. In spite of this rather blatant tension – that the movement was a woman, but the women hardly spoke – the phrase and analogy struck me quite profoundly.

Two years later, I had a conversation with another male activist, again part of the *Disobbedienti* network. Once again I was referred to feminism as a theoretical perspective I really ought to get familiar with if I were to make sense of the 'movement of movements' and its potentials. I smiled and raised my eyebrows, and so this activist, excited by my apparent interest in his own interest in feminism, jotted down a few books and essays that he believed were critical reads. I smiled again and nodded to myself, starting to make more sense of at least the cause of the ambivalence provoked by such moments.

Each time I was simultaneously compelled and disturbed by these references to feminism: excited because I too think there is something to this linking of feminism with the politics of contemporary movements. But I was disturbed because the potential was not matched in reality. I was and am continuously struck by the ways the politics and potentials of our recent movements seem to posit the possibility of a refreshingly different politics: politics that are more dynamic and sensitive, more pleasurable and immediately satisfying, better able to meld with the future worlds we would like to construct, and better equipped to theorise inadequacies. And yet, when these possibilities don't match the reality, we seem at a loss for words.

Today, although I remain inspired by the critical openness and ethos of experimentation, the willingness to theorise, analyse and reflect upon the efficacy of our actions while remaining oriented towards political transformation – traits that I believe characterise the best of our movements – I have become increasingly worried about this gap that exists between our 'new' and 'better' theories, and our lived realities.

What does it mean to see yourself as part of a movement governed by feminist and minoritarian logics when in so many of the most visible spaces, the voices and languages of women continue to be less audible? Does it matter if we have a fabulously astute and sensitive notion of what a good democratic – non-representative – politics would look like if we cannot involve more people in the conversation? Worse, is it of any use to have a great theoretical notion of the politics you want, but the very subjects you are claiming to be inspired by – that is those who have traditionally been othered, marginalised, excluded – are not present to participate in the discussion? If theoretical and reflective practice is so important to us today, even as an ethical and formal element, how do we live with such inconsistencies between our theoretical language and our experiences?

CASE IN POINT!

If you haven't yet noticed, the pages of *Turbulence* are mostly filled with pieces by men. There are very few female voices, and only one member of the editorial collective is female (me). While we can identify a lot of specific reasons this particular case of such an obvious and outrageous imbalance occurred – and even point out the fact that several women were invited and even intended to contribute articles – I think we ought to think more analytically about the issue. For despite our best intentions and the belief that we were not exclusive or biased, I don't think that the absence of many voices, especially those of women, is a coincidental or accidental occurrence. I believe it was influenced by dynamics that have everything to do with the mostly white, male editorial board, as well as cultural-structural factors harder to articulate. Moreover, I don't think going to press – despite these obvious lacks – was an obvious or inevitable choice. Rather it was the product of a certain rubric of value. One that placed greater value on both getting it out there, and on the time and effort we had put into publishing this journal regardless of the shortcomings, over the cost of having a journal with so many voices and perspectives missing. At this point, I am not making a judgment about whether that was a good choice – I am also torn – I am simply pointing to the fact that it was a choice.

While these absences are disheartening and politically very problematic, I want to see if it is possible to turn them into a useful moment to enlist those theoretico-practical capacities to engage this persistent, yet difficult to adequately define, problem within our movements. Personally, I have been struggling over how to both put into words and address concerns about the continuing dominance of male activists and masculinist politics. (Conditions that seem to be worsening – if not in a quantitative sense, then certainly in a qualitative one, because we should know better by now.) This dominance is quite obvious in the disproportionate visibility and audibility of men in many movement spaces and, more subtly, in a political modality that, despite the proclaimed absence of formulas and ideologies, remains unable to deal with specific problems and inequalities that inevitably arise in the course of collective endeavours. Not only the relative absence of female and other voices in this issue of *Turbulence*, but also the lack of women speaking at the BSF in Italy, for example. While I do not want to argue for a simplistic politics of representation, as if the mere presence of more women and more people from the global South would immediately or necessarily correspond to a better politics, I do believe that really prioritising more diversity could give us a better chance of producing such a politics!

I am also concerned that this problem is particularly insidious in the 'autonomous' or horizontalist area of the movement' that most of us on the editorial collective identify with. 'Particularly insidious' because 'we' have been so critical of NGOs, 'reformists', parties and so many others for not being more politically consistent and for failing to recognise their complicity in maintaining and even reproducing the very things our movements contest. We have touted our 'more democratic' forms of organisation, our horizontality, our lack of hierarchy, our fluid, dynamic and affinity-based organisations, while we ourselves are guilty.

Could it be that, at least in part, our inability to address these imbalances and absences is an unintended consequence of the supposedly 'new' political theories that tend to see affinity, fluidity, horizontality and lack of identity as their defining logics? Could it be that this failure has everything to do with the language and theoretical approaches of feminist and other subaltern positions we have turned to using, but without having had the experiences that produced those theoretical and practical insights in the first place? Perhaps we've misinterpreted many of these new logics – we've read them devoid of their situational contexts, forgetting what they are a reaction against, and without recognising the fact that the logics themselves are overdetermined by a sensibility that goes against any form of theorising or theoretical language that is abstracted from the messy particularities of specific situations.

EXPERIENTIAL vs ABSTRACT CONFLICT AND THEORY

Last fall I attended a four-day gathering in the north of Spain. The space was beautiful: an old Spanish church with a great deal of unused land, now home to Escanda, a live experiment in sustainable collective living. The aim of the gathering was to turn the principles and insights that have been promoted and experimented with at various counter-summits, social forums, *encuentros* and myriad other sites of our anti-capitalist activist networks, into a lasting and ongoing project where the difficulties and complexities of actually living such a politics on a day-to-day basis would be confronted. It seems fitting then that true to this spirit of taking on the challenges and difficulties we still face despite even our best-intentioned activist efforts, several women decided to organise a women-only radical (anti-capitalist) gathering. It was, to my knowledge, the first gathering of its kind: a space organised specifically and deliberately to address the 'gender problem' in the radical areas of our movements. In contrast to most women-only or feminist meetings, the gathering, also known as 'Booty Camp', self-identified first as part of the anti-capitalist/anti-authoritarian/radical-environmental networks that had been quite active in Europe for about a decade, and only secondarily as feminist. In fact, many of us arrived very critical of separatism and the exclusion of men – both in terms of whether that was good politically, and whether we would like it personally.

Despite my own concern to this end, the gathering turned out to be one of the most significant experiences I had had in years – both on a political and on a human level. The event changed me and I have not been able to engage with my political projects (or the world) in the same way since. This might sound a bit dramatic, like a cheesy harking back to the consciousness-raising groups of the 1970s where many of our mothers became empowered and from which many a legend about mirrors and masturbation come. I too felt a little overcome by how strongly I reacted to it. But in spite of the fact that I might be accused of promoting a romanticised nostalgia for a feminist movement of days gone-by, I think the parallel might be worth something, not only because of the feminist movement's widespread effects, but also because of how and why it has been so effective and how it has changed over time.

For who can deny the transformative and lasting effects of feminism? No, it hasn't ushered in an age of equality or the end of patriarchy, machismo, or capitalism, but it has profoundly transformed our social relations, our cultural norms, our very ways of being and seeing in the world. Whatever our gripes with its multi-generational manifestations – and believe me there are many – there was/is something about the feminist movement that has made it effective in truly widespread, durable and still dynamic ways: becoming a part of the 'common sense' (at least in the global North). I am not claiming that other movements like civil rights, labour, environmental and others haven't had important effects, but I do think feminism-as-movement – as an ethic and sensibility that forces people to consciously and continuously challenge dominant norms – is quite special.

Yes, feminism has certainly been rife with conflicts, rifts and problems. Open conflicts have taken place between and among women from different economic

I know that I have generalised here about the 'movement of movements' and in the process obscured important differences and the fact that many groups continue to act like the older Left characterised briefly at the outset. I have chosen to do so to highlight trends that, while certainly less valid among certain groups, still characterise a general tendency among many.

and cultural backgrounds, of different sexual and gender identities, and from and within different global regions: it is/was continuously the object of critique. However, understanding these conflicts as wholly negative is in part a problem of how we read conflict and critique. For I believe that one of the reasons feminism has been so significant, despite its most problematic manifestations, is precisely because it has managed (or been forced) to really engage the conflicts and complexities that have traversed it throughout its history: conflicts between universalism and difference, cultural values and rights, North and South, etc. And because the multiple and at times contradictory elements that comprised it have subsequently worked to transform the discursive and lived spaces of feminist articulation to life and politics. Some of the most important insights about organising across differences came as a result of the fact that women of colour, queer women, anarchist women and women from the global South (among others) critiqued, seceded and worked to change what was perceived as a hegemonic feminism. While there is no doubt that the critiques must continue and the conflicts still exist, it is also undeniable that they have been extremely productive, if not constitutive of some of feminism's most important contributions and insights into the nature of power and social change. This ethos and ability – the experience – of engaging the intersectional complexities of life despite, or even with and through, conflicts and differences without falling apart or disbanding was part of what made the Escanda gathering so powerful.

CONCLUDING THOUGHTS

I think that at their best our recent movements have the potential to have similar lived lessons emerge from encounters and even clashes among our different elements. It is that potential people were sensing when they referred to the movement as woman, as new, as exciting. However, while the language of networks, affinity groups and difference have been critical additions to our political vocabularies, they can also quite easily justify a level of complacency and comfort about remaining within our differences – as separate groups. Moreover, while we have imagined and deployed this discourse and rhetoric of difference, becoming and affect, I fear we have forgotten about the lived and messy level of experienced conflict, as well as the time and effort it takes to work through them productively. Recognising irreducible differences, attempting to work with forms of organisation that are more fluid, dynamic and based on affect and pleasure, rather than structure and strategy, are key and important elements of the 'new politics', but they are not sufficient. Nor, I would add, is theorising and calling them part of a new post-representational political logic.

Ultimately one of the most important lessons of feminism, as well as of *Zapatismo* and other sources of inspiration for our new politics, is that the most important insights come from lived and unexpected experiences, including lived encounters with difference and lived experiences of the limitations of certain political models and ideologies. If we only talk and theorise amongst ourselves we are very unlikely to come across encounters that disrupt our ways of doing and thinking. So it is not sufficient to come up with a new narrative of social change: the terms and modality of the conversation must be recast as well. However, we need more people talking, arguing even, to truly change the terms of the conversation. That is why despite my serious reservations about the choice to publish this issue of *Turbulence*, I feel that it may be OK. Or rather I hope that through its attempt at opening up an ongoing space and project of interrogation and reflection – where it may itself be an experienced object of critique – without trying to definitively capture a snapshot of, or define absolutely an adequate politics for our movements, it could turn out to be a good thing. But only if people engage with it, argue with it, add to it…

For more on the links between feminism and the politics of the movement of movements, see J.K. Gibson-Graham's *A Postcapitalist Politics*, and http://www.communityeconomies.org/index.php. Michal Osterweil lives in Carrboro, North Carolina, teaching and studying at UNC-Chapel Hill while working on various community projects. In addition to *Turbulence*, she has been active in trying to create spaces for integrating movement work with research/intellectual-theoretical production, locally and beyond. She can be contacted at mosterweil@gmail.com

Politicising sadness

Colectivo Situaciones

MORE THAN FIVE YEARS after the insurrection of that Argentine December 2001, we bear witness to how much the interpretations and moods around that event have changed. For many of us, one phase of this winding becoming was accompanied by a feeling of sadness. This text recovers a moment in the elaboration of 'that sadness' in order to go beyond the notions of 'victory and defeat' which belong to that earlier cycle of politicisation that centred on taking state power, and, at the same time, in order to share a procedure that has allowed us to 'make public' an intimate feeling shared between people and groups.

Sadness came after the event: the political celebration – of languages, of images, of movements – was followed by a reactive, dispersive dynamic. And, along with it, something happened that was then experienced as a reduction of the capacities for openness and innovation that the event had brought into play. The experience of social invention (which always also implies the invention of time) was followed by a moment of normalisation and the declaration of 'end of the celebration.' According to Spinoza, sadness consists in being separated from our *potencia* (powers-to-act). Among us, political sadness often took the form of impotence and melancholy in the face of the growing distance between that social experiment and the political imagination capable of carrying it out.

'Politicising sadness' sums up in a slogan an intention to resist: to elaborate once more what came to light in that collective experiment within a new dynamic of the public sphere, because far from shrinking or having stopped, the process which erupted then is still the fundamental dilemma of today's Argentina. In this

context and with that intention, a diverse group of collectives that shared the lived experience of political transversality in Argentina during recent years – *Grupo de Arte Callejero* (GAC – Street Art Group), the educational community *Creciendo Juntos* (Growing Together), the Movement of Unemployed Workers (MTD) of the neighbourhoods of Solano and Guernica, the communication collective *Lavaca* and *Colectivo Situaciones* – met for several weeks at the end of 2005. Inevitably, we write this text from our own perspective on what was then discussed, which implies – also inevitably – to write in tune with a dynamic that is still under way.

I. POLITICAL SADNESS

1. The logic of specialists is imposed. 'If you do arts, then don't do politics, because in the arts, we are those who handle the visual language, aesthetics, and who can say what is and what is not art.' The same kind of border is imposed from the social sciences and philosophy: a distinction has to be made between those who are fit to invent concepts and to make legitimate use of social research, and those devoted to 'political propaganda'. Thus, after a period of 'disorder' the categories of the specialists arrive to restore and resurrect classifications that – they wager – never completely dissolve. An analysis done in this way disregards the political operations that made a project, a slogan or a movement possible. There are also the experts in politics, who organise disorder in the opposite sense: 'if you do not have a clear power strategy, what you are doing is not politics, but "social activism", philanthropy, counterculture, etc.' Thus, the hybridity implicit in every creation of new political figures is intentionally confused with a costume party after which the old classificatory powers come back to distribute uniforms, ignoring the fact that those processes always have a certain irreversibility.

2. Repetition without difference. The key to the productivity (both expressive and organisational) reached at a moment of effervescence is that it enables personal and group 'fusions', along with a mixture of languages in which what matters is not the authorship of what is being created, so much as the extent to which energies come together. However, these effects cannot be repeated and reproduced outside the situations in which their meaning is rooted without becoming formulaic. Sadness arises when this uprooting occurs – but it is not perfected into a 'politics' until pure

ARGENTINA: THE DISAPPEARED REVOLUTION
by Tadzio Mueller

Que se vayan todos! ('They all have to go!') Thus went the oft-quoted slogan of the *argentinazo*, the uprising, rebellion – maybe even revolution – of 2001. The iconic images beamed across the world by the global news agencies from Buenos Aires' main square, where street fighting was raging all the way up to the presidential Casa Rosada, where social movements forced three presidents out of office in the space of two weeks, were really only the tip of the iceberg. They were moments of excess, moments of radical transformation for which years of militant and autonomous struggles had laid the groundwork.

Neoliberalism proper hit Argentina in the early 1990s. In the midst of economic crisis and hyperinflation, President Menem fixed the peso to the US dollar and pushed through a programme of privatisation, free trade and 'deregulation'. As a result, while 'the economy' stabilised, hundreds of thousands of people lost their jobs, and social conflicts multiplied. Around the mid-90s, the by now famous *piqueteros*, movements of unemployed people all around the country, made a key strategic innovation. Being excluded from the labour process, they could not go on strike. But in a post-Fordist, 'just-in-time' economy, they found that blockading roads was an effective way to mess with the economy, and pressure governments at all levels into making commitments – at the same time as the road blocks became embryonic forms of the 'popular assemblies' that would later inspire so many movements across the world.

During the 1990s, however, 'the economy' was still strong enough to satisfy the powerful Argentinian middle class, leaving the poor and unemployed tactically powerful, but strategically isolated. But by the turn of the millennium, things started to look different, because by then, large fiscal deficits and an overvalued peso began eroding middle-class incomes, as well as the jobs of the poor. Unemployment skyrocketed, and when the Asian crisis contaminated the Argentinian 'emerging market', an outflow of capital escalated into a recession that culminated in the economic meltdown of November 2001. As a devaluation of the peso loomed, the repetition crystallises and becomes established as a formula ready to be applied. The automation of the formula freezes our own capacity to temporalise the process. If the creation of time consists in opening possibilities, political sadness prevents the elaboration of lived experience as a present and future possibility. The crystallisation of the living past interrupts its elaboration as political memory.

3. Duration as validity criterion. These were common questions in the years 2001–2003: How do groups and movements relate to each other? Which common tasks can be completed through fusion, and which ones do not allow for such flexible connections? In each group or collective (artistic, political, social, etc.), questions arose about the practices taking place beyond the group, in a common outside. A

government, to forestall a run on the banks, imposed the so-called *corralito*, limiting the amount of cash that could be withdrawn from bank accounts. That was the government's death warrant.

And here we return to the iconic images of December 2001: pushed by an alliance of social movements that ranged all the way from picketing unemployed people to the irate middle-class folks who, somewhat uncharacteristically, could be seen rampaging through Buenos Aires in make-up and high heels smashing banks and fighting with police. As the movements were on the advance, the state was in retreat. As one president gave way to another in quick succession, effective power in the streets and cities seemed more and more to be wielded by the popular assemblies, people satisfied their needs in the popular eateries, and an autonomous revolution – a revolution not aimed at taking state power, but changing the world without taking power – seemed possible for the first time.

Alas, the state and capital survived, and from exhilaration the movement plunged into deep sadness. As the relative left-winger and former guerrilla-sympathiser Nestor Kirchner took presidential power and began placating social movements, movements in turn allowed themselves – or even wanted – to be coopted. And this is – perhaps – the sad source of the sadness. It does not originate from above before trickling down. It already exists deep inside the movements, and this is precisely why it is a problem. And not only in Argentina. Some would say it is more evident in North America and possibly in Europe too. The source of the sadness – there and here – is ourselves. We desire order and a sense of normality: a job perhaps, some security in our lives.

How can we understand this sadness, how can we *politicise* it? If sadness originates in our preferences for known and safe paths, then how can we escape this? How can we construct a politics *in and against* sadness, and a logic that goes beyond a simple binary of defeat and victory? By politicising sadness perhaps we can invent ways of being which embody – rather than eliminate – the multiplicity involved in creation, in the uncertainty and chance involved in the becomings that are essential components of *power-to*.

key idea to make possible those encounters was that of the 'third group': group-clusters which formed around tasks that reduced differences between the groups, at the same time as they became partners in veritable laboratories of images, words and organisation. Sadness, in its eagerness to simplify, concludes that the temporal finitude of experimentation is enough to undermine its value, making invisible both the 'common outside' and the procedures destined to shape it, thus dissipating the most profound meaning of the process.

4. Contempt for the socialisation of production. 'Anybody can produce images or concepts, forms of struggle, means of communication or ways of expression.' These statements made sense while a kind of impersonal collective production managed to disseminate procedures and socialise creative experiments. A logic of 'contagion' permeated forms of struggle, images and research, questioning the control of businesses and their brands over the field of signs. The normalising reaction arrived later to govern this viral expansion, recoding the circulating signs, once again seizing control over them.

Several procedures helped in this normalisation:

a) the emptying of collective slogans through literalisation (violently severing them from their virtualities). For example, the 'They all have to go' of December 2001;

b) the attribution of a hidden meaning as the product of 'manipulation', by the standard interpretation of phenomena of collective creation ('behind each autonomous and horizontal tendency there is nothing but a ruse of power...' or, every 'apparently spontaneous' demonstration finds its 'hidden truth' in the powers that 'orchestrate' it from the shadows);

c) the most typical prejudices of 'reactive economicism', expressed in phrases such as 'the *piqueteros* only want to earn money without working,' 'the middle class only take to the streets if something touches them in the pocket', and all the ways of reducing the subjective interplay to the economic crisis;

d) the mechanical identification of the 'micro' level with 'small', an *a priori* judgment according to which the concrete forms of the revolt are identified with a prior, local, and exceptional moment, cut off from a 'macro' ('bigger') reality, which must be run according to the guidelines that spring up from capitalist hegemony and its systems of overcoding.

5. The machines of capture. The classical dilemma with regard to institutions – to participate or to withdraw? – was in some ways overcome at the moment of greatest social energy. The resources that the collectives and movements wrenched from the institutions determined neither the meaning of their use, nor their function. On the contrary, they became cogs in a different machine, giving a different meaning to the way of relating to these institutions, without naivety, verifying in practice how that dynamic between movements and institutions depended on a relation of forces. The rise of all these extra-institutional procedures, at the same time as the movements achieved their greatest presence and voice in the public stage, aspired to a radical democratisation of the relation between creative dynamic and institution, meaning and resources. The institutions that sought to register the meaning of these novelties in general did not go beyond a partial renewal: not so much because they ignored procedures brought into play by the movements and collectives, but rather because they forgot the implications of the reorganisation of the institutional dynamic that such novelties pursued; not so much for trying to give an opposite meaning to the aspirations of the movements, as for underestimating the plane of the movements itself as the locus in which the problems regarding the production of meaning are posed.

6. Autonomy as corset. Up to a certain moment, autonomy was almost equivalent to transversality among the collectives, movements and people. That positive resonance functioned as a surface for the development of an instituent dialogue outside the consensus of both capital and the alternative 'masters' of the party apparatuses. But, once transformed into a doctrine, autonomy becomes desensitised vis-à-vis the transversality that nurtures it, and to which it owes its true *potencia*. When autonomy turns into a morality and/or a restricted party-line, it drowns in a narrow particularity and loses its capacity for openness and innovation. To the autonomous groups and movements, sadness appears as the threat of cooptation, or of giving up the search. It appears also as guilt for what they did not do, for that which they 'were not capable of', or precisely for that paradoxical process of normalisation, one consequence of which is a certain form of resentment.

7. Sudden appearance in the limelight. The mass performance that the explosion of counterpower in Argentina at the end of 2001 entailed was accompanied by a violent redrawing of the map of relevant actors, but also of the parameters for understanding and dealing with this new social protagonism. The (perhaps inevitable) spectacularisation spectacularises: it creates stars and establishes recognised voices. The consumerist relation to the 'hot' spots of conflict led to a colossal change of climate, in which the collectives and movements went from being observed, applauded and accompanied, to being suddenly ignored and even scorned, which is usually experienced with a mix of extreme loneliness, disappointment and guilt.

II. POLITICISING SADNESS
A politics 'in' and 'against' sadness cannot be a sad politics. The reappropriation and reinterpretation of the event presupposes:

1. Elaborating the event in the light of memory as *potencia*. The process does not end in defeats and victories, but we can of course be immobilised and removed from its dynamic. Learning to dismantle forms and formulae that were successful in days gone by cannot turn into a kind of repentance or simulation. Leaving behind one formula can only mean to recover all of them as possibilities, to equip ourselves with a true political memory.

2. No victimisations. Sadness only points to our momentary disconnect within a dynamic process, which need not be understood as a long phase (of stabilisation) with periodic interruptions (by the crisis of domination), but rather as a process that political struggle can go through. Not only is sadness a politics of power-over, but also – and above all – the circumstance in which the politics of power-over becomes powerful.

3. Power of abstentionism. If the *potencia* of practice is verified in the democratic sovereignty we manage to actualise in it, the politicisation of sadness can perhaps be understood as a form of prudence in which the apparent passivity radically preserves its active, subjective content. A 'despite everything' disposition that prevents us from being swept along with the current or simply conquered.

4. New public spaces. Public existence is instituted in our mode of appearing, and a way of appearing that interrogates is radically political. The institution of new public spaces in which we appear with our real questions, ready to listen to the content of the situations, does not require exceptional conditions, but a non-state institution of that which is collective. This is what the *Mujeres Creando* call 'concrete politics'.

5. The reelaboration of the collective. The collective as premise and not as direction or point of arrival: like that 'remainder' that emerges from a renewed effort to listen. The collective as a level of political production and as mutual companionship in experience. We are not talking about group formulae (of agitation or its opposite, self-help): the collective-communitarian is always a challenge of opening towards the world. It is not merely looking 'outside', in terms of a classical topology that would distinguish a 'communitarian inside' and an 'external outside', but rather the collective as complicit in the adventure of becoming a situational interface in the world.

We would like to end with a hypothesis: the ongoing dynamic in Argentina gives rise to what we could call a 'new governability' (new mechanisms of legitimating elites; innovations in understanding the relation between government and movements, between international and 'internal' politics; regional integration and global multilateralism). To prolong sadness leads to isolation in this new phase of the process.

As a 'translation' of the event, the 'new governability' distributes recognitions among the instituent dynamics and opens spaces that were unimaginable in the

Mujeres Creando ('Women Creating') is an anarchist-feminist collective based in La Paz, Bolivia.

previous phase of bare-knuckle neoliberalism. However, all this is happening along-side an effort to control and redirect those dynamics. There is no room for a feeling of 'success' for the former or 'defeat' for the latter. With the drift from political sadness to the politicisation of sadness we intend to take up the dilemmas opened by the ever present risk of getting lost in fixed, and therefore illusory, binarisms, which confront us as victory-defeat. Paolo Virno summarised what is opening in front of us this way: beyond the foul oscillation between cooptation and marginalisation, what is at stake is the possibility of a 'new maturity'.

The group Colectivo Situaciones, literally 'Situations' Collective', came together in Buenos Aires in the late 1990s and since then they have been attempting to connect thought with the new forms of politics which were emerging in Argentina. For more on the collective and what they call militant research/research militancy, see their 'Further comments on Research Militancy' and Nate Holdren and Sebastian Touza's 'Introduction to Colectivo Situaciones', both in the web journal *ephemera* and available at http://www.ephemeraweb.org/journal/5-4/5-4index.htm. This piece was translated by Nate Holdren and Sebastian Touza and appeared in *Chto Delat?/What is to be done?* #16, March 2007 (http://www.chtodelat.org/index.php?option=com_content&task=category§ionid=17& id=173&Itemid=167). It is reproduced here with some revisions by Rodrigo Nunes and Tadzio Mueller.

Worlds in motion

The Free Association

People have been saying for some time that what the movement needs are some real victories. But – it's a strange but frequent phenomenon – when movements finally win them, they often go unnoticed.

DING DONG! The Witch is dead, The Wicked Witch is dead! With the irrecoverable collapse of the latest round of trade talks, the WTO appears to be effectively defunct. The cycle of anti-summit protests of the turn of the century and beyond, and the social movements that formed around them, played a vital role in killing it off. Yet there hasn't been a general affect of victory. In fact you could even say the opposite: the 'we are winning' sentiment of the couple of years following Seattle has disappeared and been replaced by, at best, head-scratching and soul-searching. More a case of WTF than WTO.

Maybe this paradox makes more sense if we start to think of movements not as concrete blocks of people, but as a moving of social relations. Of course social relations are always moving: capital tries to pretend that it is a universal and immutable way of living, when in fact those social relations have to be re-established every day – every time we go to work, or exchange money for goods, or act in alienated ways etc. But every now and then these social relations are fundamentally challenged by our actions as we start to create new worlds. One of the places where this happens is at counter-summit mobilisations: the new worlds we create there may be temporary, or geographically limited (this is the basis of the criticism of 'summit-hopping'), but it's those same limits which make them such a rich laboratory. They produce an intensity which enables us to see this moving of social relations on two different levels, one we can call 'demands' and one we can call 'problematics'.

BE REALISTIC...

Demands are by their very nature demands to someone or something. They are demands to an existing state or state of affairs. They might be explicit – when we appeal to governments for a change in policy or we demand that sacked workers be reinstated; or they might be implicit – when we insist on our right to police ourselves. But they are always, to some extent, within the terms and sense of the thing we are trying to escape: we accept the idea of 'work' or the idea of 'policing'. Indeed if demands are ever met it is only done by further reducing a movement's autonomy. The state or capital grants the demand by recasting it in its own terms and within its own logic. This is how mediation works: think, for example, of the way 'green consumerism' is promoted as a solution to climate change. Indeed the incorporation of demands almost always takes the form of a counterattack – the cost of action on climate change, for example, will always be shifted on to us (eg road pricing, green taxes). As the saying goes, be careful what you wish for...

But it's not as simple as saying that all demands lead to empty recuperation ('bigger cages, longer chains...'). Those bigger cages also give us more room for manoeuvre. And it is partly because demands operate on the foreign territory of representation that we fail to recognise the achievement of demands as victories. They appear as the actions of our opponents, the product of their good sense and not our activity. But we need to dig a little deeper to see what's really going on. In many ways demands involve a freezing of (a) movement, an attempt to capture what we are and raise it to the level of representation. But as a crystallisation, they also contain our logic within them, like a fly trapped in amber. It's similar to the way the product of our work is sold back to us: sometimes it's hard to see the social history buried within the latest government announcement.

There's a second reason why we find it hard to see victories in the realm of representation as winning. There's a time-lag to this process: when we stormed through Seattle in 1999 chanting 'Kill the WTO!', we felt like we were winning, but it wasn't until 2006 that the WTO fell to to its knees. By the time demands are 'met', movements have moved on. And this isn't just a question of time: it's also to do with speed. During intensive moments, like counter-summit mobilisations, we can move so incredibly fast that a few days seem like years. Think of the way we arrive at a convergence centre or camp site: to begin with, it's just a featureless field where we struggle to find our bearings, yet in the space of a few days, we have transformed it into a new world.

...DEMAND THE IMPOSSIBLE!

But demands are just one moment that social movements move through. They are necessarily lop-sided and partial, because they operate on a terrain that is not ours.

We're more interested here in the movement on the level of 'problematics'. Unlike demands which are implicitly vocal or static, problematics are about acting and moving. If demands are an attempt to capture who we are, then problematics are all about who we are becoming.

Social movements form around problems. We don't mean this in a simple functionalist fashion, as if there is a pre-existent problem which then produces a social movement that, in turn, forces the state or capital to respond and solve the problem. Rather, social movements produce their own problematic at the same time as they are formed by them. How does this work in practice? Firstly there has to be a moment of rupture that creates a new problem, one that doesn't fit into the 'sense' of contemporary society – this is the grit that the pearl forms around. The Zapatista uprising is one example, but we could just as easily refer to climate change or border struggles. With this rupture come a whole new set of questions, new problems which don't make sense and which don't have a simple solution. As we try to formulate the problematic, we create new worlds. This is what we mean by 'worlding': by envisaging a different world, by acting in a different world we actually call forth that world. It is only because we have, at least partially, moved out of what makes 'sense' in the old world that another world can start to make its own sense. Take the example of Rosa Parks who simply refused to move to the back of the bus. She wasn't making a demand, she wasn't even in opposition, she was simply acting in a different world. It's the same with the 'anti-globalisation movement': no sooner had we come into being as a social force, than we were re-defining ourselves as an alter-globalisation movement. In many ways, we were in a novel position of having no-one who we could put demands to. How else could we act if not by creating another world (or worlds)? And who would create it if not us? But first we have to create that 'us'…

And here's where we return to the realm of demands, of crystallising, because the process of creating this new agency (this new 'us') also involves acting at the level of 'demands', and this can be an extremely productive moment. The rupture itself

Social movements have no 'right' to world. In fact any autonomous problematic automatically takes them into the sphere of becoming revolutionary. And that problematic can come from a 'No' just as much as from a 'Yes'. From capital's perspective, autonomous demands are always partial and one-sided ('selfish' even) because we refuse to take its logic into account. There's a great moment from the English Revolution of the 1640s, when the Levellers are threatening to turn the world upside down with their demands for equality. Sir Thomas Fairfax, Commander-in-Chief of the Army, loses it and asks them, 'By what right or power do you make these demands?' There's a silence before they reply, 'By the power of the sword, master Fairfax, by the power of the sword.' More than three centuries later, at the height of anarcho-punk, the band Crass re-worked this in slightly more direct terms: 'Do they owe us a living? Course they fucking do!'

can take the form of a demand, maybe a simple 'No!' That can give a movement an identity by providing a static position around which people can orient themselves – a public staking-out of ground within which an expanded social movement can cohere. This is exactly what happened with summit protests over the last decade. Most of us didn't go to Seattle, yet an identity was forged there which we could loosely relate to. That identity was strengthened and deepened as it moved through Gothenburg, Cancún etc. In other words, summit protests were not only conscious attempts to delegitimise the meetings of the rich and powerful. They simultaneously legitimised our worlds and widened the space for worlds governed by logics other than that of capital and the state. Summit protests played a vital role in creating a new 'us', an extended 'we'.

On another scale we were part of exactly the same process at the 2003 G8 summit when there was a mass road blockade at Saint-Cergues: the 'No!' of the front line barricade created space in which a new body could cohere and start to develop consistency. We created new knowledge (tactics for dealing with tear gas and pepper spray); we developed new ways of decision-making (for maintaining food and water supplies, and working out when and how we would withdraw); and we extended the problematics (blocking side roads, making connections with local residents).

This move from opposition to composition, from the level of demands to the problem of practice, is never easy. The UK anti-poll tax movement, for example, never managed to find its own autonomous consistency – when the government finally backed down in 1991, the movement imploded. We had been held together by our 'No!' – it's what allowed us to stand together – but without the emergence of 'Yeses' we were simply unable to move. But trying to bypass the level of demands altogether is equally fraught. One of the criticisms of the mobilisation against the 2005 G8 summit was that we were too easily out-manoeuvred by a state-orchestrated campaign (Make Poverty History) which was used to make demands 'on our behalf'.

Inevitably this moving has to take into account things that appear to be outside of it, like the actions of the state or the deployment of a police helicopter at Saint-Cergues. So we move in response to new developments, to evade capture. But there is also an internal dynamic caused by the new enriched material that has cohered around the original 'grit'. This new material has its own new properties and might then find itself with new internal problematics. At a macro-level we can think here of the debates about the black bloc or the issue of violence after Genoa, where a whole new set of questions were posed and everything moved on. Or we can look at how the idea of convergence centres at summit protests has been developed to embrace

The anti-poll tax movement is reckoned to be the biggest mass movement in UK history, involving some 17 million people: over a period of about 18 months a huge non-payment movement emerged, culminating in a month of town hall demonstrations and riots in March 1990.

a whole practice around social centres, whether rented, owned or squatted. These centres, however temporary, are one space within which movements can thicken and start to develop a consistency.

BENEATH THE PAVEMENT...

There is a bigger problem here. There's a relation between our autonomous movements (inventing new forms, throwing up new problematics etc.) and the effects those movements have on capital and state and their mechanisms of capture. But

Perhaps another way to think of this is in terms of measure. Demands operate in a field of certainty, what we can call an extensive realm. It's the realm of 'things', which can be defined, counted, negotiated and partitioned. 'You want a 0.25% tax on all foreign exchange transactions? How about 0.1%? Or how about just within the G8?' etc etc. They are essentially static, which is what makes them easy to measure and capture. Problematics, on the other hand, operate in a realm of moving desires and subjectivities. They are dynamic processes that are indivisible, and it's in this intensive aspect that changes happen. Think about a demonstration: you can measure it by the number of participants, or the value of damage caused. Looked at this way, a demonstration of 5,000 is half as effective as one of 10,000. But the level of anger, or the feeling of powerfulness, or the degree of collectivity are intensities that can't be measured in the same way.

there is a danger that we stay trapped within this relation and never manage to break free. We can never entirely evade capture, but we can try to develop techniques to postpone or minimise it. And this is where counter-summit mobilisations have proved essential.

In everyday life it's quite easy to see the world of demands, of things, but it's more difficult to work out what's going on underneath. We can glimpse traces of the underlying dynamics in spectacular eruptions (Paris 1871, Barcelona 1936, Seattle 1999, Oaxaca 2006…) or by looking at the realm of demands and seeing what's reported in the press, or how states act. Summit protests can shatter this everyday equilibrium and make the intensive realm spring to life. We can see commodities for what they are – dead. We get a sense that this is *real*, this is *life*. And we can see more easily what social movements are made of. This has profound consequences. At these times it becomes obvious that our movement isn't a movement of us (activists vs others) but a moving of social relations, an unfreezing of all that is fixed. This moving of social relations is like the breaking of an ice-floe: it has no edges or boundaries ('this group is in our movement, this group isn't' etc), or rather the boundaries are always in motion; the moving ripples through everywhere – absolutely everywhere. This is the affect of winning that we experienced in Seattle and elsewhere. We felt we were winning because we weren't 'we' any more; maybe we'd even abolished any idea of a 'we', because there was no outside, no 'us' and 'them' any more. In fact this slippage in 'we' is reflected in this text: the meaning of 'we' goes from 'us the authors' to 'you the readers' to an extended 'we' that defies measurement. Moreover what we do cannot be limited to what is consciously decided: sometimes we 'do' things behind our own backs.

But this shattering of the everyday also forms a new point of rupture, a new jumping-off point. And this can be one of the ways we can escape the twin apparatuses of capture the state deploys. First, at the level of demands, the state attempts to incorporate us into its logic of sense. Here we can think of how the police tried to incorporate the land-squatted Camp for Climate Action into its own logic of legality by offering to be 'helpful' and just wanting to walk around the camp once. This 'offer' was initially accepted as there was a need for the camp to feel a certain sense of security. But there was a price to pay: when we move on the terrain of legality (whether 'illegal' or 'legal'), we are within their sense not ours. Allowing the police on site set a precedent and it became impossible to refuse constant patrols, without forcing a new rupture. When we instigate that break, and follow the logic of our deepening problematics, we come up against the other pole, the state's machine of outright repression. The danger is that we get trapped in this pincer of incorpo-

The Camp for Climate Action took place in the summer of 2006 near Selby in Yorkshire, UK. More info from www.climatecamp.org.uk or see Paul Sumburn's article on page 37 .

ration/repression, and our activity in response to either diverts us from our own autonomous movement.

We come full circle here: the problem that faces us again and again is the risk of being trapped in the logic of capital and the state, whether as radical reformers, summit protesters, workplace activists or whatever. Capital always takes its own limits as universal ones, but in truth those limits are 'theirs', not ours. The only way for autonomous social movements to avoid this dance of death is to keep breaking new ground. In this sense, winning, in the realm of problematics, is just the gaining of extended problematics, as our experimental probing opens up ever-wider horizons. Or more prosaically, all that movements can ever get from 'winning' is more movement. And that's why we keep getting drawn back to counter-summit mobilisations like Heiligendamm: they are one of the places where the movement of movements can break the limits of its formation and ask its own questions.

Alex, Brian, David, Keir, Nate and Nette freely associated to produce this piece, but we were helped along the way by countless others, especially people around the CommonPlace social centre in Leeds, UK (www.thecommonplace.org.uk). As ever, we've pinched ideas from all over the place, but some of our sources should be named. The opening quote is from 'Biggest victory yet over WTO and "free" trade. Celebrate it!' by Olivier de Marcellus (http://info.interactivist.net/article.pl?sid=06/08/18/0417238&mode=nested&tid=14%3Cbr%20/%3E). The extensive and intensive concept is from Deleuze and Guattari's *A Thousand Plateaus*. Paul Hewson's article in *Shut Them Down!* is a thorough account of the politics behind Make Poverty History and the lessons to be drawn from it (www.shutthemdown.org). The exchange between Fairfax and the Levellers is lifted from Ian Bone's brilliant *Bash The Rich* (Tangent Books). Comments, criticisms and communication welcome: info@freelyassociating.org. Our virtual home is www.freelyassociating.org

Commonism

Nick Dyer-Witheford

IT HAS BEEN EIGHT LEAN YEARS for the movement of movement since its Seattle high point of 1999. Since September 11th 2001 many activists' energies have been directed to opposing the invasion and occupation of Iraq, other conflicts in Afghanistan and Lebanon, and abuses of civil liberties and media truth. But the war on terror has also had a deadening effect on oppositional hopes and imagination. Or so it seems to me, an academic in Canada whose political energies have recently been absorbed opposing his university's making tanks for the US Army. Comrades are engaged in labour organising, post-carbon planning, the self-organisation of the homeless, municipal elections and other projects. But the optimistic sense of another world as not only possible but probable, imminent, has given way to something more sombre. Even in this no-longer-frozen North, the upsurge of popular movements and governments in Latin America is an inspiration. Otherwise, however, horizons have contracted.

Global capitalism appears – by profit levels – robust. Cascading ecological calamities, suddenly peaking oil, another 9/11, or an uncontrolled unwinding of US-China relations could all destabilise the world system. But not only are such scenarios contingent; it is uncertain they would be to the advantage of progressive movements. Neo-fascists, fundamentalists and martial law capitalists could be the beneficiaries, unless intellectual and organisational preparation lays the ground for a better alternative.

It therefore seems important to renew the discussion of what we want: to think through not just what we are against, but what we are fighting for (and hence who 'we' are), and to consider what might be plausibly achieved in present circumstances. Many movement activists and intellectuals are currently addressing this task, here and in other forums. My contribution will be to propose and discuss 'commonism'.

'Commons' is a word that sums up many of the aspirations of the movement of movements. It is a popular term perhaps because it provides a way of talking about collective ownership without invoking a bad history – that is, without immediately conjuring up, and then explaining (away) 'communism', conventionally understood as a centralised command economy plus a repressive state. Though some will disagree, I think this distinction is valid; it is important to differentiate our goals and methods from those of past catastrophes, while resuming discussions of a society beyond capitalism.

The initial reference of 'commons' is to the collective lands enclosed by capitalism in a process of primitive accumulation running from the middle ages to the present. Such common agrarian lands are still a flashpoint of struggle in many places. But today commons also names the possibility of collective, rather than private ownership in other domains: an ecological commons (of water, atmosphere, fisheries and forests); a social commons (of public provisions for welfare, health, education and so on); a networked commons (of access to the means of communication).

Let us extend this term 'commons' in a slightly unfamiliar way. Marx suggested capitalism has a cell-form, a basic building block, from which all its apparatus of commerce and command are elaborated. This cell form was the commodity, a good produced for sale between private owners.

If the cell form of capitalism is the commodity, the cellular form of a society beyond capital is the common. A commodity is a good produced for sale, a common is a good produced, or conserved, to be shared. The notion of a commodity, a good produced for sale, presupposes private owners between whom this exchange occurs. The notion of the common presupposes collectivities – associations and assemblies – within which sharing is organised. If capitalism presents itself as an immense heap of commodities, 'commonism' is a multiplication of commons.

The forces of the common and the commodity – of the movement and the market – are currently in collision across the three spheres we mentioned before: the ecological, the social and the networked.

In the ecological sphere, decades of green struggle have disclosed how the market's depletion and pollution of nature destroys the common basis of human life. This destruction runs from pesticide poisoning to clear-cutting to species-extinctions. What now highlights this process is global warming. The prospect of chaotic climate change destroying agriculture, water supply and coastland around

A computer, say, is a 'rival' or 'rivalrous' good. My possession of it deprives you of it. But goods like software are 'nonrivalrous'. A piece of software can be copied costlessly and therefore we can both use it simultaneously.

the planet (although, as usual, most devastatingly in the South) throws into sharp relief the scale of ecological crisis. It also definitively displays the inadequacy of the 'free market' and its price system as a social steering system. The scale of intervention now necessary is indicated by George Monbiot's recent ten-point plan to address global warming: targets for rapid reduction in greenhouse gas emissions, borne primarily by the developed North; individual carbon quotas; high-energy efficiency building regulation; banning and taxation of high-emission devices; diversion of public funds from 'defence' and road building to clean energy and public transport systems; freezes and reductions in air travel and out of town superstores. One can debate every point in this prescription. But if Monbiot is even close to correct, the remedy required exceeds anything the market, even as 'green business', can do. It demands regulation, rationing and major public investment. Global warming (along-side other ecological crises, from fish stocks to water tables) puts back on the table precisely what neoliberalism attempted to erase: massive social planning.

In the social sphere, the red thread of labour, socialist and communist movements traces the attempt to replace the class divisions of capitalism with various forms of common wealth. Defeating this challenge was the mission of neoliberalism. It has had great success. Precisely because of this, intensifying global inequalities are now having universal consequences. The afflictions of what Mike Davis calls the 'planet of slums' cannot be walled off from the planet of malls. They return as disease (HIV/AIDS and other pandemics) or insurgency ('terror'). In this context, two movement initiatives have picked up the issue of 'common wealth' in innovative ways. One is the movement of 'solidarity economics' focused on cooperative enterprises of various sorts and associated with the success of the Latin American Left. I discuss this later. The other is a set of proposals and campaigns around what is variously known as a 'basic' or 'guaranteed' income, which, by assuring a modest level of subsistence, saves human life from utter dependence on a global labour market. Such programmes also address feminist political economists' point about the market's systemic non-reward of reproductive work (care of children and households). Basic income was initially proposed in the global North West, and in that context can be criticised as a supplement to an already-affluent welfare state. But basic income has recently appeared as a policy initiative in Brazil and South Africa. Some groups have proposed and costed a basic global income of $1 a day. Insignificant in a North American context, this would double the monetary income of the one billion plus people officially designated as living in extreme poverty. If one thinks this utopian, consider the $532 billion 2007 US defence budget. Again, there are more than enough debates to be had about a global basic income: it might, for example, be better conceived not as a cash economy payment but as a basic 'basket of goods' or a guaranteed global livelihood. But the failure of trickle-down market solutions to poverty and inequality (even in the midst of a global boom), and the increasing extremity of the consequences, creates opportunities for new common-wealth activism.

In the network sphere, the failure of the market appears in a different way – as capital's inability to make use of new technological resources. Computers and networks have created the increasing capacities for extremely fast, very cheap circu-lation of communication and knowledge. These innovations were made outside of the market, in a strange encounter between public funded science (the military/ academic sector) and libertarian (and sometimes revolutionary) hackers. Capital's contribution has been to try and stuff these innovations back within the commodity form, realising their powers only within the boundaries of information property and market pricing. But digital innovation has persistently over-spilled these limits. Peer-to-peer networks and free and open source software movements have taken advantage of the possibilities for the reproduction of non-rivalrous goods and collaborative production to generate networked culture whose logic contradicts commercial axioms. The movement of movements realised these potentials in its early weaving of what Harry Cleaver called an 'electronic fabric of struggle,' using the internet to circumvent corporate media and circulate news, analysis and soli-darity. Increasingly, however, free and open source software and P2P constitute an electronic fabric of production, equipping people with a variety of digital tools for everything from radio broadcasts to micro-manufacturing. Capital is attempting to repress these developments – through incessant anti-piracy sweeps and intellectual property (IP) battles – or co-opt them. But alternatives beyond what it will allow are expressed in 'creative commons', 'free cooperation' and 'open cultures' movements contesting the intellectual property regime of the world market.

All three domains – ecological, social and networked – evidence major market failures. Each illustrates the failures of a commodity regime, though in distinct ways. Ecological disaster is the revenge of the market's so-called negative externalities, that is, the harms whose price is not, and indeed cannot be, calculated in commercial transactions. Intensifying inequality, with immiseration amidst plenitude, displays the self-reinforcing feedback loops of deprivation and accumulation intrinsic to market operations. Networks show the market's inability to accommodate its own positive externalities, that is, to allow the full benefits of innovations when they overflow market price mechanisms. Together, all three constitute a historical indictment of neoliberalism, and of the global capitalist system of which it is only the latest, cutting-edge, doctrine.

Also in all three domains, movements are proposing, as alternatives to these market failures, new forms of commons. These too vary in each domain, although, as I will argue in a moment, they also overlap and connect. In the ecological sphere, commons provisions are based primarily on conservation and regulation (but also on public funding of new technologies and transportation systems). In the social sphere, a global guaranteed livelihood entails a commons built on redistribution of wealth, while solidarity economies create experimental collectively-managed forms of production. In the case of the networked commons, what is emerging is a commons of abundance, of non-rivalrous information goods – a cornucopian commons.

Of course, these three spheres are in reality not separable; any life-activity resonates in all three, so that, for example, ecological and networked activities are always social commons – and vice-versa. Indeed, my argument is that the form of a new social order, commonism, can be seen only in the interrelation and linkage of these domains – in a circulation of the common.

Marx showed how in capitalism, commodities moved in a circuit. Money is used to purchase labour, machinery and raw materials. These are thrown into production, creating new commodities that are sold for more money, part of which is retained as profit, and part used to purchase more means of production to make more commodities… repeat *ad infinitum*. Different kinds of capital – mercantile, industrial and financial – played different roles in this circuit. So, for example, the transformation of commodities into money is the role of merchant capital, involved in trade; actual production is conducted by industrial capital; and the conversion of money capital into productive capital is the task of financial capital (banks, etc).

We need to think in terms of the circulation of commons, of the interconnection and reinforcements between them. The ecological commons maintains the finite

Harry Cleaver's piece 'Computer-linked social movements and the global threat to capitalism' is available at http://www.eco.utexas.edu/~hmcleave/polnet.html. George Caffentzis discusses neoliberalism's 'plan B' in his chapter in *Shut Them Down!* (available at www.shutthemdown.org).

conditions necessary for both social and networked commons. A social commons, with a tendency towards a equitable distribution of wealth, preserves the ecological commons, both by eliminating the extremes of environmental destructiveness linked to extremes of wealth (SUVs, incessant air travel) and poverty (charcoal burning, deforestation for land) and by reducing dependence on 'trickle down' from unconstrained economic growth. Social commons also create the conditions for the network commons, by providing the context of basic health, security and education within which people can access new and old media. A network commons in turn circulates information about the condition of both ecological and social commons (monitoring global environmental conditions, tracking epidemics, enabling exchanges between health workers, labour activists or disaster relief teams). Networks also provide the channels for planning ecological and social commons – organising them, resolving problems, considering alternative proposals. They act as the fabric of the association that is the *sine qua non* of any of the other commons.

Let's suppose that a publicly-funded education institution (social commons) produces software and networks that are available to an open source collective (networked commons), which creates free software used by an agricultural cooperative to track its use of water and electricity (ecological commons). This is a micro model of the circulation of the common.

This is a concept of the common that is not defensive, not limited to fending off the depredations of capital on ever-diminishing collective space. Rather it is aggressive and expansive: proliferating, self-strengthening and diversifying. It is

It might be objected that, in Marx's description of the inner workings of capitalism, the commodity is presented as possessing a self-creating, self-reproducing dynamism, and that the fact that some commons – especially the ecological ones – are finite would prevent such dynamism. But this objection confuses a qualitative with a quantitative issue, or, more accurately, a social dynamism with a dynamism of production. The model proposed here, of circular interaction between ecological planning, basic income and open networks, argues for the expansion of the social relations of the commons: a secure level of livelihood for global populations reduces the need for constant environmentally destructive growth; open networks enable ecological and income planning to be democratically debated, monitored and revised in an ongoing collective process of general intellect; planning in turn ensures the infrastructures and access for this process. Whether or not this social dynamism would be productively dynamic – whether it would produce more or less goods – is a different question, to which the answer is surely 'more of some, less of others': less SUVs, energy mega-projects and luxury mega-homes, more public transport, solar panels and decent basic housing. But the commons form, like the commodity form, is first and foremost a social relation, and its most important dynamism lies in the alteration of collective logics.

also a concept of heterogeneous collectivity, built from multiple forms of a shared logic, a commons of singularities. We can talk of common earth, a common wealth and common networks; or of commons of land (in its broadest sense, comprising the biosphere), labour (in its broadest sense, comprising reproductive and productive work) and language (in its broadest sense, comprising all means of information, communication and knowledge exchange). It is through the linkages and boot-strapped expansions of these commons that commonism emerges.

This concept has a clear affinity with the movements of solidarity economics that emerged from Latin America and are now gaining increasing attention in North America and Europe. Broadly defined, these aim to link self-managed and worker-owned collectives, cooperative financial organisations and socially-responsible consumption practices to create expanding economic networks whose surpluses are invested in social and ecological regeneration. Euclides Mance, one of the theorists of the movement, writes of such 'socially based cooperation networks' reinforcing their component parts until 'progressive boosting' enables them to move from a 'secondary, palliative or complementary sphere of activity' to become a 'socially hegemonic mode of production'. This type of activity – to which, I think, basic income programmes would be complementary – seems to resemble the sort of cell-growth of commons envisaged here.

Mance says that this process is 'not about the political control of the State by society', but about 'the democratic control of the economy by society'. Latin American activists will, however, be much better aware than I that the creation of grass roots alternative networks goes better with protection, support and even initiation at a state level. For that reason, one might think of the circulation of the common as involving not only a lateral circuit between ecological, social and networked domains, but also a vertical circuit between new subjectivities, autonomous assemblies (solidarity networks, cooperatives, environmental and community groupings) and governmental agencies.

The movement of movements has been tacitly split between autonomist and anarchist groups, with strong anti-statist perspectives, and socialist and social democratic movements, committed to governmental planning and welfare functions. Rather than either repressing this tension, or replaying it *ad infinitum*, it may be both more interesting for both sides and closer to the real practice of many activists to think about the potential interplay of these two poles.

Commons projects are projects of planning: the regulation of carbon emissions (or other ecological pollutants), the distribution of a basic income (or of public health or education) or the establishment of networked infrastructures are all extremely difficult on any large scale without the exercise of governmental power.

The nightmare of previously existing socialisms was the assumption by this governmental planning power of despotic bureaucratic forms. The antidote is a pluralistic planning processes, which involves a multiplicity of non-state organisations capable of proposing, debating and democratically determining what directions governmental planning takes. Thus a requirement of 'commonist' government is the cultivation of the conditions in which autonomous assemblies can emerge to countervail against bureaucracy and despotism, and provide diversity and innovation in planning ideas. Planning and anti-planning have to be built into each other: there should always be, to quote Raymond Williams, at least two plans.

As George Caffentzis has pointed out, neoliberal capital, confronting the debacle of free market policies, is now turning to a 'Plan B', in which limited versions of environmental planning terms (e.g. pollution trading schemes) community development and open-source and file sharing practices are introduced as subordinate aspects of a capitalist economy. But the question hanging over this encounter is which logic will envelope and subordinate the other: who will subsume who?

Commonism scales. That is, it can and must be fought for at micro and macro, molecular and molar, levels; in initiatives of individual practice, community projects and very large scale movements. If the concept is at all meaningful, it is only because millions of people are already in myriad ways working to defend and create commons of different sorts, from community gardens to peer-to-peer networks.

In my view, however, a commonist project would gain coherence and focus by agreement on a set of high level demands to be advanced in the ecological, social and network spheres at the national and international level, demands that could be supported by many movements even as they pursue other more local and specific struggles and projects. These demands might include some briefly discussed here: for example, a guaranteed global livelihood, carbon-emission rationing and adoption of free and open-source software in public institutions.

Such demands would be radical but not, in a negative sense, utopian. Success would not mean we had won: it is conceivable that capitalism could persist with these provisions, although they would represent a planetary 'New Deal' of major proportions. But achieving them would mean, first, that the movement of movements had won something, averting harms to, and bestowing benefits on millions; and, second, it would mean that we were winning: these altered conditions would create opportunities for new collective projects and waves of organising that could effect deeper transformations, and the institutions of new commons.

Nick Dyer-Witheford is an Associate Professor in the Faculty of Information & Media Studies, University of Western Ontario, in London, Ontario, Canada, and a member of the Counter-Stryker collective opposing military-academic-corporate collaborations. He is currently studying the contemporary usefulness of the young Marx's concept of 'species-being.' He can be reached at ncdyerwi@uwo.ca

The crazy before the new

Complexity, critical instability and the end of capitalism

Kay Summer and Harry Halpin

Even in a cosmic or geological time perspective there's something unique about our century.

— Martin Rees
2006 Presidential Address,
UK National Academy of Sciences

CAPITALISM: A COMPLEX SYSTEM

The staunchest believers in capitalism are frequently anti-capitalists. This is not as paradoxical as it seems. Many believe that capitalism is capable of recuperating any form of resistance or crisis. This makes it invincible, and therefore the best one can do is write hand-wringing critiques of capitalism, which is what many anti-capitalists seem to do. Here we highlight an entirely unexpected source of optimism for life beyond capitalism: insights from the most radical shift in science in the late 20th century, the emergence of complexity theory. Complexity theory and, more broadly, a non-linear view of the world, may offer some potentially profound insights, particularly for those of us wondering where to put our energies to create a different social system.

Complexity theory is relevant to any system that links many different parts in a dynamic network, that is, a network which itself changes over time. One of the features of these systems is that they are governed by non-linearities. This means that sometimes a small event causes a small reaction in the system, but at other times a similar event can have a massive effect. It is easy to argue that capitalism is a complex

113

dynamic system governed by non-linear dynamics, and so complexity theory may be a good way to understand the social world we live in.

Capitalism is complex, the result of the interaction of over six billion people. Capitalism is dynamic, as the rapid changes in working practices and the bewildering expansion of commodities attest. Capitalism is a 'system', that is, a network with nobody 'in charge' (just witness the failed historical attempts to direct capitalism). Lastly, capitalism is highly non-linear. Take the unexpected financial crises, which changed life for millions in Argentina in 2001. These were sparked by a few financial investors removing their money from the country. Yet investors remove money from countries every day with usually negligible effects.

COMPLEXITY MADE SIMPLE

Complex regenerating dynamical systems maintain their own structure above all else, even while there is a great deal of change to the structure's component parts. A human body is a good example of a regenerating system. We change our component parts – our cells – over time, but we retain our major features – our internal organs, skin colour, and so on. Thus change – and simultaneously continuity – is the norm. Such complex regenerating systems require two major components. First, there must be many different interacting elements that compose the system. Second, the law of entropy, also known as the second law of thermodynamics, must be overcome. The law of entropy states that systems degrade over time, losing their organisation to become simpler. To counteract that tendency there must be regular incoming supplies of materials or energy into the system. This is everyday experience: human bodies need food, water and oxygen, otherwise our bodies become rapidly less and less complex, dying and eventually decomposing to simple molecules.

Regenerating complex systems are therefore open, materially and energetically – whether they are self-organised or human created (like the internet) – and this always requires regular new inputs of materials or energy. Hence, these systems are maintained away from equilibrium. Or rather, they are maintained away from a static equilibrium. Take a simple example: a child on a swing. This dynamical system does have a static equilibrium point, but it's not very interesting and it's certainly not much fun! Once the child is swinging this introduces dynamism to the system. With a fairly regular supply of energy, a new state of dynamic equilibrium can be maintained. Biological organisms, ecosystems, capitalism, the internet are all much more complex dynamical systems: given inputs of energy or materials they too never stabilise to a static equilibrium with their environment. They are constantly being pushed away from such equilibrium by the flows of energy and materials. For the internet to be maintained, for example, broken computers must be replaced – materials and energy need to flow – otherwise it decomposes and stops being a complex system.

Complex systems possess emergent properties: they are more than the sum of their parts. A person is more than a pile of water, carbon, nitrogen, and other molecules; a person is more than a collection of macromolecules or cells or organs. The internet is

more than a collection of computers. This is because the configuration of the connections is important. Complex systems involve many connections between components that form loops of interaction. This contrasts with many hierarchical systems where the interactions between the various components are deliberately minimised. It is the feedback loops involving these connections that can change the system as a whole. So-called negative feedback loops tend to keep the system in its current state, while positive feedback loops may push a system to a new state, or new type of system.

This brings us to another important point: regenerating complex systems often have multiple stable states. We can explain this by imagining a topographical map with valleys and hills. Now imagine a ball rolling around, in constant motion. This is our complex system. Most of the time, the ball will stay in the same valley; various forces may push it away from the valley bottom, but it will tend to roll back towards this same valley bottom. The whole valley, which surrounds the stable state that is the valley bottom, is known as a basin of attraction. It would take a massive disturbance, or a tiny disturbance of just the right kind, to set off a positive feedback loop, to get the ball to roll right out of that valley and into another, another basin of attraction. Such major changes, from one valley to another, do occur, but they are usually rare, often requiring several simultaneous changes. Moreover these major changes, from one valley to another – known as phase transitions – are often preceded by periods of 'critical instability', during which the system is under great strain. It can lurch widely, exhibiting seemly chaotic behaviour, before settling into a new, more stable, state. These periods are known as bifurcation points, because it appears that the system could go one way or another. The ball is balanced precariously on a ridge and there are potentially several valleys it could descend into.

One example of a phase transition is the switching of the entire Earth between cooler glacial periods and warmer inter-glacial periods (as we live in now). Others are the socio-economic transitions from hunter-gatherer society to agriculture and animal husbandry, and from feudal or peasant societies to the capitalist mode of production. Often what revolutionaries are looking for is such a phase transition.

For highly complex systems there are an unknown and unknowable number of these basins of attraction, or *attractors*. They are 'attractors' precisely because, regardless of where the system is at a given moment in time, it will tend towards one of these states. Some systems eventually converge on one state, but many complex systems, called chaotic or periodic systems, cycle through a set of these attractors, and their trajectory among them seems to be impossible to predict as an apparently insignificant change can move a system from one attractor towards another. These attractors are often called *strange attractors*. Needless to say, a system whose trajectories can hardly be predicted cannot be directed or managed. But some events can be predicted as being much more likely to cause the system to move towards a new attractor, although the exact nature of that attractor is unknown. These events usually involve radically changing the energy or material going into a system, or radically changing the connections of the constituent parts within the system, including adding or removing many connections altogether.

Is this theory useful? Think of the radical and global-scale changes we humans have experienced; the rapid increase in energy use and material production; the explosion of communications, via mobile phones, the internet and easier and easier long-distance transport. These massive increases in both energy and materials and connectivity, alongside the looming ecological crisis, suggest potentially optimal conditions for a phase transition which would, by definition, be the end of capitalism.

SOCIAL ORGANISATION: ALWAYS A COMPLEX THING

Human social organisation has always been, and always will be, complex and dynamic. This is because it involves a large number of people interacting in a network. Historically there have been two – possibly three – stable states of social organisation, that have attained and maintained near global dominance: hunter-gatherer societies, subsistence agricultural societies and, if it lasts, capitalism. We don't include the many highly hierarchical large-scale civilisations – the feudal system of medieval Japan, Mayan civilisation or classical imperial systems like ancient Rome – because although such societies have appeared and disappeared regularly across the globe, none has achieved global dominance. This suggests that these civilisations were not stable states. It suggests authoritarianism is not a functional survival strategy, because the attempt is always to control people based around rigid social organisation, rather than allow for the continuous regeneration and development of the system as its constituent parts – human beings – and its environment change.

116

What is interesting about the phase transitions from hunter-gathering to agriculture and from agriculture to capitalism is that both transitions were associated with a major increase in the energy and material input into the system, and with an increase in the number and density of connections within human society. Take the switch from hunter-gather societies – humanity's first stable-state, which spread to every continent and lasted for at least two million years – to subsistence agriculture. Occurring eight or nine times, seemingly independently, some 8–12,000 years ago, this transition contained the double dynamo (positive feedback loop) of the cultivation of crops and population growth: crop-cultivation increased the seed available to produce more crops that could be saved during lean times, which in turn allowed a larger human population to live, which itself enabled more people to plant more crops. This feedback cycle continued, increasing global human population rapidly, from a mere quarter of a million people 8,000 years ago to around 600 million before the European conquest of much of the world in the 16th century AD. And not only did population increase. Relative to population, farming societies had many more connections than the relatively small bands of hunter-gatherers in loose networks. In turn, the switch to capitalism included the dynamo of the generation of profit for reinvestment, also increasing material and energetic inputs over time. And the invention of the commodity – which heralded the birth of capital – led to a framework involving the circulation of goods and services on a scale hitherto unimaginable, and again, a consequent increase in the number of connections between individual humans and different environments.

Now consider two recent phenomena affecting human society: the massive increase in connections, as a result of the internet and other communications technology, and the rapidly escalating global ecological crisis. These are the kinds of changes on a scale that seem to us possible major contributors to a third phase transition in the organisation of life in human history. We finish this article by turning to these.

THE GLOBAL ECOLOGICAL CRISIS
The production of goods and services for sale in a competitive market, where the profits are reinvested in further production to be repeated ad infinitum, contains a central flaw. Ever-expanding production requires ever-expanding resources, leading to a chronic crisis with no exit: the global ecological crisis. In short, capitalism has always relied on infinite expansion, and there can be no infinite expansion on a finite planet. After 500 years capitalism is ceasing to be a good survival strategy.

Capitalism is attractive because as a survival strategy it works (though people have also been utterly repelled by it as well). You remain quiet, work hard, play the game and you will be rewarded with enough food to eat, shelter and, most likely, a marriage resulting in children. However, as the material substrate of the system collapses, capitalism as a survival strategy is becoming less and less attractive. In more and more people's minds, the 'cost-benefit' will shift. In order to survive, people must, and will, develop alternatives to capitalism. Their (our) very survival will depend upon it.

There are two criticisms of this argument. The first comes from capitalists, particularly those who promote 'green capitalism', a brilliantly creative misnomer. At best, green capitalism could slow capitalism's decline, extending its lifetime for maybe a few decades. But green capitalism is still capitalism: the requirement of accumulation – of work, material and energy – without end remains. The second objection comes from radicals who argue that threats such as climate change are in fact nothing but the usual rhetoric of imaginary crises – scare-stories to further justify the exploitation of workers and violent oppression of revolt. It's true that some crises are illusionary crises; but others are real. This goes back to our opening line, that anti-capitalists are often the staunchest believers in capitalism. Capitalism is not some latter-day god that can change physical laws. We *do* live on a finite planet.

GLOBAL CONNECTIVITY
Connections between people are radically changing. Communication technologies and mass-transport reshape our connections – literally, as in the physical ability of one part of the system to connect to another. As the number of connections increase, the system becomes ever more complex, and it's thus more likely that small changes are magnified. The combination of digital computing with communication lines produced the archetypal network of networks: the internet. This more than any other technological infrastructure has led to radically increased connectivity, rapidly increasing further due to its convergence with mobile technologies and their rapid spread through even the rural Third World. In periods of stability people use such technologies to do the things they normally do in stable situations: flirting, say, but via text messaging. But when our very survival is at stake, or when we catch a glimpse of a much better future, people can use these technologies for extraordinary goals, to mobilise globally in a sophisticated manner never before seen in history.

The original round of the anti-globalisation movement was in effect the result of new connections between movements in the global South and those in the global North, brought together by the internet. As these technologies fall into more and more hands, as is rapidly happening, people who have little at stake in the current social system will use their newfound ability to connect for their own purposes. Collectively, people will be able to react to events much faster than in previous times; and new social order can emerge spontaneously, via the connections people choose to make, rather than order imposed by leaders.

WHAT NEXT?
We've mentioned the massive increase in connectivity. We've mentioned the awesome increase in material and energy inputs that are now forcing capitalism up against external environmental limits. Beyond these factors, the sheer schizophrenia of our world leads us to believe we are living through a period of *critical instability*. This

term is used to describe a complex system that is behaving wildly, and seeming chaotically. Critical instability usually signals the first detectable stage of a bifurcation point, that point at which massive systematic changes start. We are lurching towards a new-yet-unknown system or systems. Only one generation in forty or fifty may have the chance to live through a phase transition in human society, and more importantly, have the chance to actually create the new society. This spectre of collapse is both terrifying and exciting!

When uncertainty about the future is in the air, dreams of past stable social systems often re-emerge. Think of the swathes of people in the Middle East who desire to return to a feudal theocracy or of the desire of so-called 'primitivists' for humans to become hunter-gatherers again. So we should remember that although other worlds are possible (and also likely), some are worse than this one. Fortunately, both feudal theocracy (because it's highly authoritarian) and hunter-gather society (because it means the death of 90% of humanity) are extremely unlikely. There are just too many connections and too much material (including 6.6 billion human brains) and energy (again all those people), for such scenarios to be plausible. The phase transition we're approaching will be to something new and never seen before.

One potential basin of attraction is eco-fascism. An elite will use modern tools of control and command to instate some socially authoritarian global economy that is materially steady-state for those outside the elite. In times of limited resources, people live in fear of not having enough resources, and some dividing lines for the haves and have-nots would be used. This would be more brutal than the have/have-not divides of today. We can glimpse this attractor in contemporary struggles around migration, which will only become more intense as global ecological crisis cause massive population movements. Eco-fascism would be an especially duplicitous enemy, as many of its advocates use anti-capitalist rhetoric. Eco-fascism is unlikely to become a stable attractor – it is bound to fail eventually – due to its closed nature that destroys connections. But in the meantime the cost to humanity and the planet would be immense.

A second possible attractor would be decentralised and cooperative communities whose relations are based on affinity – that we all ultimately share the same biosphere – that maintain a high-level of connectivity with each other. Unlike fascism and strangely like capitalism, this attractor bases its power and resilience on the strength of its connections. This form of social organisation is perpetually open, always seeking new connections; and in the spirit of complexity theory, and unlike previous revolutionary movements, it embraces no determinism. The logic of autonomy allows the components of the system to optimise their own connections, and so connect to people, materials, passions, and places in manners that takes optimal advantage of material and energy flows. Production is linked to a logic, not of growth, but of satisfying collective needs through 'commons' – as outlined by Nick Dyer-Witheford elsewhere in this issue. Production and decisions about production are made via direct democracy – which maximises connectivity. Moreover, this highly flexible system of autonomy, collectivity and commons may well allow us to confront the ecological crisis.

We have reasons to be optimistic. The question of whether capitalism will still be the dominant mode of production at the end of this century is almost always answered in the negative. Capital's current trajectory cannot continue. Complex systems can change within the blink of an eye. The global ecological crisis usually invokes pessimism. But, perhaps paradoxically, it also provides hope. There are currently more optimal conditions for rapid shifts in human social organisation than there have been for probably two if not five hundred years. Of course, we cannot know what form this new social system will take. But we should remember that free will and human innovation and creativity are the hidden variables. What may appear to be minor actions can, in these hyper-connected times of critical instability, have consequences magnified beyond imagination.

Kay Summer and Harry Halpin have both had longtime involvement in the movement of movements and some of its precursors. They earn their wages by doing scientific research, some of this involving trying to better understand non-linear systems and ideas. This is their second collaborative piece on non-linearity and social movements; the first was published in *Shut them Down!: The G8, Gleneagles 2005 and the Movement of Movements* (2005, www.shutthemdown.org). You can get in touch with the authors at kaysmmr@yahoo.co.uk and harry@j12.org

Move into the light?
Postscript to a turbulent 2007

It's nighttime and a man is crawling around on his hands and knees, looking for his car keys underneath a lamp post. A woman comes along and starts to help him. After they've been searching together for a while the woman asks the man: "Are you sure this is where you dropped them?"
The man replies: "No, I think I dropped them somewhere else."
"Then why are we looking here?" she enquires.
"Because this is where the light is."

AT THE BEGINNING OF 2007, the Turbulence Collective commissioned 14 articles from around the global 'movement of movements', asking authors: "What would it mean to win?" We edited their responses into a newspaper and printed 7,000 copies, most of which were distributed at the mobilisation against the G8 summit in Heiligendamm, Germany, in June. A few months later, we want to return to the question of winning.

As we resume our search it's no surprise that we keep coming across the problem of *visibility*. When we think about winning, our eyes are drawn to things that are highly visible or easy-to-measure, such as institutional or legislative change, the opening of a social centre or an increase in membership. That's where the light is. But we also need to assess victories in the less tangible though just as real realm of possibilities. Winning in this realm may involve increased potential, changes in perception or patterns of behaviour. Yet these seem to exist at the very edge of the luminous zone.

This problem leads into another: our experiences create their own luminosity and consequently their own areas of darkness. When we think about winning we are drawn to movements, people and events that are familiar to us; and we have expectations about how things should turn out if they are to constitute a victory.

So how can we overcome our night-blindness once we move beyond the familiar? In a sense this ability to look outside ourselves was key to Heiligendamm.

HEILIGENDAMM: A DIFFERENT REPETITION?

In many ways, this year's G8 summit on Germany's Baltic coast was much as we had expected it to be: a repetition of previous counter-summit mobilisations from at least Seattle onwards (Prague, Gothenburg, Genoa, Evian, Cancún, Gleneagles…). Each of these events saw a broad constellation of actors brought together in productive cooperation. Each opened up a space and set in motion processes of contamination (often behind people's backs) that were key to the politicisation of a generation of militants. On the one hand, people launched practical challenges to the legitimacy of global command (the rejection of dialogue, the blocking of roads into the summit); on the other, commonalities and mutations were produced, in the camps and convergence centres, during debates and actions.

However, previous summit mobilisations had already shown us the limits of such events. After Seattle, in 1999, it became clear that the affect produced in mass street actions would not translate automatically into everyday practices of transformation. Two years later Gothenburg and Genoa showed the price that would be paid by a movement for entering into a logic of near-symmetrical conflict (imprisonment, injuries and death). And Gleneagles 2005 showed the extent to which the desires of a movement could be captured and turned against itself, with 300,000 marching for the G8. So if many had already seen the limits of summit mobilisations, and Heiligendamm had always promised to be a repetition, surely the last thing it was going to be was *different*?

Sometimes, however, what appears like mere repetition is not really a repetition at all; at least not in the sense that it is simply the same thing taking place over and over again. So rather than return to a particular point in a cycle ('Bringing Seattle to Germany', for example), the point at Heiligendamm was to start anew with an unforeseeable process of becoming – one that would hopefully go beyond the achievements and limits of the past. Less a repetition that sought to mimic, more a new experiment in the production of politics; overcoming rather than reaffirming existing identities.

In the run-up to the summit, the groups involved in the organisation of the protest underwent something of a reconfiguration. They took some significant steps towards becoming a more genuine 'movement of movements'. A common 'choreography of resistance' was built and designed by a wide spectrum of groups – from the autonomous radical Left through to people organising inter-confessional prayer sessions against poverty. While more radical elements attempted to set the terms of the coalition (a rejection of the G8's legitimacy alongside a toleration of diverse forms of action), there was a willingness to compromise and come to common

agreements as to which forms of action were appropriate where and when. In this way Heiligendamm moved beyond the principle of 'diversity of tactics' that had become commonplace, and returned to the earlier process of cross-pollination. Instead of different political currents engaging in different forms of action – in a spirit of solidarity but without jeopardising their own identities – the work developed in Germany was in the direction of a 'becoming-other, together'. This meant collectively devising and carrying out forms of action new to all, actions and alliances that took people beyond their comfort zones towards the practical constitution of new commons, and therefore new common potentials.

WHAT'S THE SCORE?

While Heiligendamm wasn't a quantitative high-point in the history of the counter-globalisation movement (in terms of numbers, Genoa and Gleneagles were both around four times the size), in other respects it did seem that a new *qualitative* high was reached. It was a 'victory' because it was a reconstitutive moment, not least for the German Left. But something was missing from this affect of victory: the sense of having *defeated* the other side. Sure, we scored some successes against the police and summit organisers with our mass blockades. But German chancellor Merkel won legitimacy by appearing to force 'the recalcitrant Americans' into an agreement on climate change. And the G8? It is celebrating the Heiligendamm summit as one of its most successful ever. It managed to create the impression that the leaders of the world are tackling the 'global challenge' of climate change.

When the G8 first became the target of massive protests towards the end of the 1980s, it was relatively easy to point to the in-built illegitimacy of its activities. At the 1999 Cologne summit, when it clumsily responded to actions by social movements in the global South (and some northern NGOs) by passing debt-relief programmes, hardly anyone took them seriously. But the G8 reinvented itself. It stopped being just a place for the major capitalist powers to hammer out differences and became a media-circus that presents itself as the only forum that can deal with global concerns. In other words, as the G8 came under attack, its very purpose became the re-legitimation of its global authority. And it learnt its lessons well. At Gleneagles, a big NGO operation sponsored by the UK government saw 300,000 people turn out, not to demonstrate against the G8, but to welcome and 'lobby' it in favour of debt relief and aid for Africa.

The initiative lost in Scotland – where the protests were hijacked by an efficient PR offensive – was successfully regained in Heiligendamm: the explicit goal of all major actions was the delegitimation of the G8. The problem however was that the G8 had once again moved on, now seeking to draw legitimacy by seeming to respond to widespread concern about climate change. And this is where we (got) lost. The actions carried out in Germany failed to convey a political challenge to the G8's relegitimation on the issue of climate change, which had become a new key terrain of struggle.

How did this happen? One reason is that there isn't yet an overarching 'alternative' narrative to the newly greened global capitalist agenda: however bad their story may be, there is nothing else on offer. But the problem runs deeper than that. The G8's narrative on climate change solutions is a fiction, just as it was on making poverty history. But we can't counter this with a fiction of our own: at the moment we don't know how to 'solve' climate change. None of us can see far enough or clearly enough. All we can do is move from one puddle of light to another.

WHAT'S IN A LIMIT? CAPITAL, CRISIS AND CLIMATE CHANGE

It's no coincidence that talking about the G8 should lead directly to talking about climate change. For movements, it represents the possible emergence of a new focus, as shown by the buzz in public opinion and events such as this year's climate camp in the UK which, it seems, will be repeated in Germany, the US, Sweden and elsewhere in 2008. From the perspective of governance and capital, it is becoming a key element in the management of the global system, both at the level of decision-making and of political legitimation, not to mention new market niches. In the space between movements and governance, it exemplifies the ambiguity and complexity of the question of 'winning'. If the whole emphasis of environmental activism over the last few years has been on raising awareness about the threat of climate change, then 2007 must be seen as the year when 'we won'. The issue is now everywhere, and everyone, politicians and big companies included, talk about it.

Yet it is precisely this victory that could prove to be a defeat. Global concern about climate change must be given a new form if it is to actually affect the state of things (that is, radically reduce carbon dioxide emissions in a short time-frame). In part this means constructing a new story, one that can stop the issue being turned into a huge profit-making opportunity for capital. Without this, it's easy to see climate change being used to unleash a new regime of austerity on the governed, and to excuse measures like increased 'security' and border controls as geopolitical tensions rise. But if the fight is to be more than a public opinion dispute – one where we're always on the back foot – then it has to also take place at the level of production and social reproduction.

It's common to think of climate change as a technical-environmental problem that calls for a technical-environmental solution: the problem is too much carbon dioxide going into the atmosphere, so the solution is to reduce these emissions to 'acceptable' levels via technological innovation, government legislation and the public 'doing their bit'. The difficulty with this is twofold. First, almost everything we do is bound-up with fossil fuel use and the resulting CO_2 emissions: from travelling to work to phoning-in sick so we can watch DVDs. Second, the cuts required (some 60–90% before 2050) are so large they require sweeping changes, and cannot be solved simply by the world's environment ministries getting together.

An alternative way to understand climate change is in terms of metabolism. The Earth's metabolism, its ability to process carbon, runs at a slower speed than the metabolism of contemporary capitalism. The economy is on a collision course with the biosphere. Here we are talking about a limit to the expansion of capital and a possible crisis of accumulation.

For capital, limits are peculiar. Capital has an internal dynamic of expansion which must be satisfied, so limits must be ignored, subverted, side-stepped, or otherwise overcome. And the secret of capital's longevity lies precisely in its ability to use limits and the crises they engender as a launch-pad for a new round of accumulation and expansion. A good example of this dynamism is the emergence of the so-called Keynesian/Fordist phase of capitalism. The high levels of organisation of the industrial working class in the first half of the 20th century – not only the Russian Revolution but intense struggle worldwide – appeared as a limit to the expansion of capitalism, threatening not only to halt accumulation but to destroy the system once and for all. The welfare state was a direct result of these struggles, but it was also a way of neutralising this threat. And capital's greatest feat was to strike a productivity deal which actually transformed this limit into the engine of a new phase of capitalist growth.

What does an analysis of the generic response of capitalism to limit-crises tell us about likely responses to climate change? There's no doubt that climate change is a limit which presents as many opportunities as dangers to capital. Many are jumping at the chance to take this new limit, this potential crisis, and turn it into a new motor for accumulation. Look at the clamour for buying and selling rights to emit carbon: carbon credits, carbon offsets, Tradable Emissions Quotas, carbon futures. And then there's green consumerism: green cars, solar panels, green home make-overs. Could climate change inject new dynamism into the global economy? Are we looking at a new, 'green' phase of capitalism, where the atmosphere is opened up like cyberspace was in the '90s? It's possible. And it's also obvious that it's unlikely to cut carbon emissions radically!

A capitalist solution will look, well, like capitalism. Just as the effects of climate change are uneven, having a far more devastating effect on the poor – look at the impact of Hurricane Katrina in New Orleans, or the east Asian tsunami on Aceh – so almost all the current crop of solutions will also work to reinforce existing hierarchies. Most 'green' taxes will increase the price of basic goods and services, limiting mobility and access to food and heating. Access to travel, food and comfort all tied in to possession of money? No news there, of course: just the rules of the game as we know it. Except now they will be justified on the grounds that they're necessary in order to save the planet. Expect 'green capitalism' to be a new regime of austerity and discipline, imposed on the poor more than on the rich in the name of the 'greater good'.

THE EYE OF THE STORM

But capitalism is neither all-conquering nor invincible. If climate change might open up a moment of crisis, it's worth trying to understand what its dynamics might be.

One key aspect is the variable of time, understood in two different ways. First, there is a problem of time lag. The outcomes of different decisions, in climate change terms, are felt decades later. Due to the thermal inertia of the climate system there is a huge temporal mismatch between cause and effect. This means that if the impacts of climate change become 'out of control', they may stay that way for several decades. Second, all the scientific evidence points to the urgency of the problem. If we are to avoid the 'tipping points' – points at which climate change becomes potentially irreversible and catastrophic for the majority of the Earth's population (the death of the Amazon rainforest being one example) – emissions have to be drastically reduced within the next decade.

There's a positive side to this sense of urgency. A lot of the 'awareness-raising' activism of the last ten years worked with no time variable whatsoever; it addressed 'the public', a general 'other' who needed to be 'informed' of what is going on. Because of that, there were no general deadlines, no overall calendar, no sense of escalation, no particular goals; when everything is always happening 'right now', there is no time as such. The urgency of climate change raises important questions which only exist because of the time variable; they are questions of strategy and tactics.

And here we return to the question of winning. For instance, some suggest that nothing this big can be done with such little time, and the best that can be done is start preparing now for the worst. We may as well extinguish the lights and blithely head off into the darkness. Others have said that the problem is so massive and so pressing that only a centralised body is capable of tackling it. Faced with the abyss of the unknown it's tempting to turn back to the comforting light of the state. But this harsh glare blinds as well as illuminates.

Take the example of air travel. The growth in aviation is clearly a massive environmental problem, so it's easy to get lured into supporting new taxes on flying, say, or even seeing people who fly as part of the problem. But focusing on this issue might make it harder to see some of the other dynamics at work. By restraining our autonomy or strengthening capitalist and state institutions, some climate change solutions may hinder other struggles and make it harder to tackle the larger causes of climate change. What is needed is a lens – an approach or ethic – that allows us to pose the question of how climate change politics can resonate with other struggles. Not because movements need an explicit, *conscious* connection in order to resonate with one another; they don't. But we do need to bring to light resonances and dissonances. Once we can see the paths, they're easier to follow.

While we have to be wary of being blinded by the glare of the state, we can't just close our eyes to it. So how can we relate to institutional forms? Perhaps recent events in Latin America can provide some clues.

CHANGING THE WORLD *BY* TAKING POWER?

The last few years have seen the rise and establishment of governments in different shades of red across Latin America. Chávez's Venezuela, Morales' Bolivia and Lula's Brazil have generated the most international discussion. But there's also Rafael Correa's Ecuador, Tabaré Vasquez in Uruguay, the return of Daniel Ortega in Nicaragua and, more contentiously, Michelle Bachelet in Chile and the Kirchners in Argentina. These national processes are not independent, but share two related themes: first, the neoliberal model has run out of steam in the region; and second, the movement of movements has managed to make its mark at an institutional level. But what are we to make of this institutional success? Some people see these electoral victories as the only concrete result of those post-Seattle years. In this sense, 'winning' would also be the defeat of the 'movementism' of that period: confirmation that it is impossible to 'change the world without taking power'. By this logic, all that is left to do is to ensure that, once in power, the parties and groups that rode on that wave of resistance are able to produce change within institutional constraints. Further, these parties and groups that have ascended to power must also be forced where possible to transform institutions in ways that make them more permeable to this 'pressure from below'. It is taken for granted that such pressure can only fulfil its role if it is capable of being translated into institutional forms.

While we shouldn't underestimate the advances taking place across so much of Latin America, it's worth pausing to consider the implications of this view of social change.

First of all, it's important not to gloss over some important differences among these countries. It is only the case of Morales that directly corresponds to the picture of a growing wave of resistance leading to electoral victory. The history of Bolivia in the last ten years has been punctuated by moments of radicalisation that were always recuperated into the existing political system, only to be denied resolution again. As the episodes of resistance became more frequent and powerful, they forced the systemic rearrangement that carried Morales' MAS (*Movimiento al Socialismo*) to power. In Brazil's case, a similar wave took place in the 1980s, and was beaten at the polls three times until Lula was elected. By then, the Workers' Party (PT) had become the translation into party politics of a movement on the wane (with the possible exception of the landless workers movement, the MST). In Venezuela, despite a diffuse anger at the impermeability of the institutions and at the policies implemented in the 1980s and '90s, there was no movement as such. Chávez has acted as a catalyst for an intensification of mobilisation and participation which is unheard of in Venezuelan history. It remains to be seen whether he was only the catalyst, or whether he has now become the pillar without which it could all come crumbling down.

More importantly, the idea that these electoral victories are the only practical result of the last decade is flawed on two related counts. First, it assumes that 'politics' only takes place in the institutional places where we normally look for it. This discounts a whole series of networks, infrastructures, knowledge, cultures and so on – a diffuse web of collective intelligence and memory that is always active in one way or another, always producing change, and crystallising as an antagonistic force at crucial points. The escalation of resistance in Bolivia before the MAS victory is a good example of this. What 'disappeared' after each flashpoint would 'return' bigger and stronger. And it could only do so because it had never gone away.

Second, it ignores that fact that movements, as long as they keep moving, have ways of effecting and producing change that do not need to pass through, or even be recognised by, institutional politics. They can do this by, to give a few examples, transforming public discourse, by making legislation unenforceable, or simply through their power of self-management and autonomous self-constitution.

WHAT IF THERE WERE A NEW CYCLE OF STRUGGLES AND WE WEREN'T INVITED?

This question of the power of movements brings us back to where we started. As the *Turbulence* newspaper explained, we had three main reasons to produce a publication for the G8 summit in Heiligendamm. The first, very pragmatic, was that it would be relatively easy to distribute to a wide readership. The second was that in our experience summit mobilisations are spaces where people are more open to other ideas.

The third includes a more complex wager. Since Seattle, summit mobilisations have been the most visible face of the movement of movements, the way its role as a global force is most explicitly manifested, and also the times when its strength and orientations can be gauged. But by the same token it's at summit mobilisations that all the movement's potential limitations have been most apparent.

On one level, the wager was what everybody asked themselves on the way to Heiligendamm: how socially relevant, big, transformative is this event really going to be? Will this be a last gasp, a new beginning, or neither? And, equally important, whatever it is, how will we recognise it?

But if we criticise those who only recognise change on the institutional level, are 'movementists' not similarly guilty of looking for answers in the usual places? Here we are again writing of summit protests and counter-summits. Perhaps the impasse of the last few years has arisen precisely because people have failed to see answers in the places they searched, and did not start looking elsewhere. However hazy our image in the mirror has always been, have we not become too enamoured of it to actually have a look around? What if there were a 'new cycle of struggles', and we were not invited?

Think about what happened in the French *banlieues* in autumn 2005 (and appears to be re-emerging as we write). Anyone on the 'established' Left – parties, trade unions, 'activists'; if you know who we are talking about, you belong in this category! – who claims that those who revolted are 'with us' in any strong sense would be guilty of appropriating someone else's struggle by misrepresenting it. Sure, they fight against many things that we oppose. But let's look at the established Left's reaction to them, along its three general lines. Either the *banlieues* are brought into a ready-made framework, and become the 'proof' of some 'new stage of capitalism'. Or they signify the terror of a social dissolution that requires state intervention to redistribute wealth and access to opportunities in the long term (but possibly also to police them in the short term, so as to prevent civil war). Or they represent a romantic, abstract 'other' whose tough, uncompromising radicality – the poster image of revolution – is paid back with equally abstract solidarity.

If this is all 'we' – parties, unions, 'movementists' – have to offer, let's recognise that we are part of the problem. Even the most 'radical' members of the established Left could only interpret the *banlieues* as an eruption of pure negativity, a 'force of nature' rather than the work of real people. For the mainstream politician, it is the face of fear: we're on the verge of civil war! For others, it's in itself nothing, but as an unknown quantity it can fit anywhere in the theory: 'See, it confirms our predictions!' The latter simply eliminates the event; whatever else happened would mean just the same. The first two recognise an event, but see it as something so beyond any explanation that it can only be a harbinger of the end of the world (something to celebrate or lament, depending on your taste).

All three positions ignore the fact that, if the *banlieues* pose a problem, it is a problem made of flesh and bones. The banlieues reveal a gap in our knowledge: for as long as that gap is not filled by *banlieusards* – met on their terms, introduced by their own voices – 'we' feed into the game that excludes 'them'. Worse, by posing as interpreters of those to whom we don't speak, 'we' actively reproduce this game. And there is political currency to be gained, even for the most marginal left-wing groupuscules, by pretending to speak on behalf of those outside the gates. The real challenge, then, lies in effectively opening the gates to those outside. Or better, in tearing down the wall altogether. But this kind of coordination can only take place through actually working with actual people. There is little to be gained by flattering ourselves that abstract feelings of 'solidarity' matter in any real way.

Another example: for over a year now, different cities in Spain have seen a unique movement coalesce around people's frustration with the impossibility of getting 'dignified housing' in the face of rampant property speculation. The movement began when, at the height of the anti-CPE protests in France, an anonymous individual sent out an email calling for a day of protest for 'dignified housing'. The email did the rounds, and on the arranged day hundreds of people – from cab drivers to hairdressers, as well as 'activists' – took to the streets. By the second self-convoked day of protests there were thousands involved. Since then a number of local assemblies have been created, many of which are still going.

The reactions of 'activists' to this housing struggle have been interesting. They ranged from confusion ('How come there is a protest and I don't know who called it?'), to a desire to fade into the background ('In the assembly everyone is equal, people shouldn't expect us to have anything special to say'), to a recognition of how their specific knowledges could be useful ('Well, I organised a protest once, and I realise it works better if we do it like this…'). People with less of a history in politics, on the other hand, sometimes seemed to go in the opposite direction: famously, the Madrid assembly at one point discussed whether it should subscribe to a protest it had not called – 'Now we're the space in which the movement is organised, so we should be the only ones to decide these things'; 'But didn't this all begin with a spontaneous demonstration in the first place? Didn't you attend that?'; 'I did, but that was before there was the assembly!…'

All of this underlines the point that, no matter what meaning we give to the label 'movement of movements', it offers no guarantees. 'Seattle' or 'Cancún' or 'Heiligendamm' don't mean 'we' are the be-all, end-all of social change. In fact, they don't even mean 'we' exist. And to pretend we do, and that history is exclusively ours to make, can only make us blind to where we fit. (And if we *fit* somewhere, it means logically we are not the *whole*.)

MOVE INTO THE LIGHT?

This 'thought travelogue' that we have tried to establish – from Heiligendamm to Latin America, from the politics of climate change to the *banlieues*, to the movement of movements and back again – saw us start with a question and a few thousand papers to distribute, and come across a few themes and problems that just won't go away.

We've started with the theme of visibility because it highlights the relation between movements and their dynamic of self-reproduction. It's relatively easy to think of movements grappling with institutional politics, like the electoral experiments in Latin America, or the social forum process, or recent attempts to realign social centres across Europe. Depending on your perspective, these are examples of movements 'selling out' or 'growing up' or 'being recuperated'. But all three positions make the mistake of seeing institutional forms as somehow *separate* from movements. Or put another way, all three see movements as discrete bodies, with an 'inside' and an 'outside', rather than as an endless moving of social relations.

As movements move, they constantly throw up new forms of organisation and practice which are constantly settling and consolidating. Of course this can be problematic: once established, identities and rituals can become huge obstacles to change. But this doesn't mean that movements die as soon as they begin to take root, or as soon as they move into the light of exposure. This process is also a way in which movements cast *their own* light. The 'movement of movements', for example, is an institutionalisation of a certain moment of struggles, with Seattle as one of its highlights. It has also helped to generate a whole series of other institutions, which have developed their own dynamics. Summit protests, for example, took place around the world, each building on the other with subtle and not-so-subtle modifications. As that cycle of protest seemed to wane, the social forum process took off, constructing a different kind of experiment. After the 2007 World Social Forum in Kenya, heavily sponsored and controlled by NGOs, many felt that this process itself had come to an end. But a few months later the US Social Forum showed that it's possible to organise something that would not last just a few days but would produce effects in cross-pollinating and coordinating different struggles.

In fact the recent *encuentros* hosted by the Zapatistas brought this point home forcefully. They offered an encounter between, on the one hand, 'movement' visions of autonomy, horizontalism and non-hierarchical practice and, on the other, a real attempt to make these visions work on the ground – under threat of attack by paramilitaries and surrounded by hostile forces. Many 'movementists' got an insight into the functioning of the 'Juntas of Good Governance', a long-term experiment in self-government by the Zapatista autonomous municipalities. A startling aspect of this was the experience of being in a space where men with guns – the EZLN – are on your side. But if we're serious about producing change in visible and tangible ways, how is that possible without creating institutions of one kind or another? How else are we *really* going to create other worlds?

But there's a second theme of light and luminosity. When we asked the question 'what would it mean to win?', we were deliberately not asking for a ten-point programme. We didn't want 'illumination'. Instead we wanted to assert a politics that recognises that no one has the solution, that changing the world is, at least in part, a process of 'shared investigation', and that as a first step we can begin to ask the same questions. This is a world apart from the old-school politics of certainty, which is dominated by polemical confrontations, where differing political identities and approaches are pitted against each other, recreating identitarian or ideological niches.

Of course the idea of total illumination is a fantasy. But it's a very tempting delusion, one tied up with the myth of total knowledge. If you stare at the sun for long enough, an after-image will be etched into the back of your eyelids. After the G8 seized the issue of climate change, some concluded that we just need the *right* narrative, one that shows only we have 'the answer'. Rather than adopt this approach, with all its overtones of dual power and counter-hegemony, it seems more productive to take another lesson from Heiligendamm. As people prepared to block the roads

A conversation with the Turbulence Collective

Sasha Lilley, with Michal Osterweil and Ben Trott

Sasha Lilley The essays in this book were put together in newspaper form for distribution at the G8 summit in Heiligendamm, Germany in 2007. What response did you receive from counter-summit activists?

Ben Trott The immediate feedback we received in Heiligendamm was overwhelmingly positive. To be honest, I had my doubts that people would find the time to read through the paper whilst so much was going on. But it seems that somehow they did.

Ahead of the summit, some members of Attac, with John Holloway, organised an event in Berlin, as well as another series of workshops at one of the protest camps in Rostock. Some of the articles from the paper – now included in this book – formed the basis for discussion at these events.

During the summit itself, thousands of people took part in three days of mass blockades, organised by Block G8. While we were taking part, we distributed copies of the paper. The police had been fairly brutal in trying to stop people reaching the blockades, but once the roads had been taken there was very little confrontation and people found various ways of occupying themselves. This included reading the paper. We were really amused to see what else people did with the collection of texts. Some people, on their way to the blockades, wrapped the papers around their arms to protect themselves from the police's batons. And during the blockades, one group managed to turn the paper into a giant game of Twister.

The paper was also distributed around some independent bookstores and radical social centres in the UK, the US and Germany. Demand soon outstripped supply, so we were really pleased to get the offer to collaborate with PM Press on this book.

People have also been really great in terms of translating some of the articles in the first issue of *Turbulence*. Most of these can now also be found on our website.

So generally speaking, the paper we distributed at Heiligendamm was well received. However, my feeling is that it was more the *problematics* addressed, rather than the 'answers' offered up by the articles which allowed it to find the resonance it did. I think there is now a general recognition that the counter-globalisation movement finds itself at an impasse. To take the time to ask ourselves what it would mean to win – or to be winning again – seems like an extremely timely task to busy ourselves with.

SL You argue that Left victories can be complex and contradictory, as capital often responds by co-opting oppositional demands so as to open up new avenues of accumulation. How does this process tend to work – and is there a way for us to organise to impede it?

BT This is one of the issues that we sought to address by problematising the notion of measuring success in the first issue of *Turbulence*. And it's something we explore in relation to the current struggles around climate change in *Move into the Light?*

There's a quote from William Morris, the 19th Century English socialist, writer and founder of the Arts and Crafts Movement, which explains this process brilliantly. He suggests people "fight and lose the battle, and the thing they fought for comes about in spite of their defeat, and then it turns out not to be what they meant, and other men have to fight for what they meant under another name."

Quite appropriately, the quotation forms one of the two opening epigraphs to Michael Hardt and Antonio Negri's book *Empire*. I say appropriate because I think one of the greatest accomplishments of their book has been to bring together the Italian Marxist tradition of *Operaismo* and a particular strand of French post-structuralism, i.e. that of Foucault and, more importantly, Deleuze and Guattari. The book was not the first time that the two traditions had resonated with one another, but it is certainly the most accomplished effort to date towards developing a productive synthesis between the two approaches.

Operaismo famously inverted the traditional approach to analysing the relation between labour and capital, in which the former had often been regarded as a passive, reactive victim of the latter – whether that be through territorial expansions embodied through colonial or imperialist projects, or transformations at the point of production. What *Operaismo* did was turn this on its head and explain capitalist development as a constant process of *reacting* to the struggles of the working class. Every upsurge in struggle was met by an effort at 'decomposing' the working class, attacking its organisational forms and reorganising both the mode of production and regulation. The most recent and generalised examples of this would be the move from the era of 'Fordism' to 'post-Fordism'.

Towards the end of the 1960s and beginning of the 1970s, there was a massive upsurge in resistance by the social subjects which constituted the Fordist-Keynesian reality. From workers involved in mass production (characterised by the industrial factory conveyor belt) and students (who were subject to a similar process of massification, through the so-called 'proletarianisation' of education), to women's movements and the increasing power of anti-imperialist and anti-colonial struggles the world over.

Capital's gradual and uneven response to these struggles was the move towards what is generally labelled 'post-Fordism' and neoliberalism. Large production plants were broken up and replaced by smaller scale, networked, more flexible processes exemplified by the developments at Toyota and Benetton (this was, of course, a process which was most obvious in the global North, but similar, less drastic tendencies have also been observable in the South). Trade was liberalised and regulation – both domestically and internationally – was reduced, increasing capital's mobility. Restrictions were placed on the ability of trade unions to act and intervene.

As a result, 'old' organisational forms were decimated (i.e. 'decomposed'), providing huge challenges, for example, to workers seeking to improve their lot. And in those locations where workers were able to organise, capital was increasingly able to simply pack up and move elsewhere.

Post-Fordism and neoliberalism, however, have their ambivalences. Whilst the former, for example, in many ways represents an *intensification* of exploitation – to the extent that it tends towards requiring that our entire subjectivities are put to work for capital – it is in many ways a result of the demands of earlier movements for a more creative way to spend one's time than working 9-to-5, five days a week on a conveyor belt, or pulling a lever. So to stick with the Morris quote, post-Fordism in many ways was the defeat of the struggles of Fordist social subjects, whose victory – in part – came about after all, in the sense that change was forced. But the precarious, neoliberal reality of today is certainly not the communist or socialist utopia that the workers and students of '68 were fighting for. The task which faces us now, then, is to continue this struggle (albeit, perhaps, under a different name!).

Deleuze, particularly in his collaborations with Guattari, describes a similar dynamic in their deployment of a number of different concepts. What they describe as the 'war machine', perhaps surprisingly, does not stand for any kind of 'military-industrial-complex', but rather resistance *against* the state. The war machine operates as something that resists centralisation and everything sedentary, it sets in motion a process of transformation (what they call 'becoming'). In response, the state always attempts to appropriate and/or capture this resistance, using it for its own ends.

There are strong parallels here with Deleuze's concept of 'desire', a productive and positive force which embodies a potential for transformation against that which seeks to repress it. At the same time, it is never entirely 'free' from codification by the powers of social regulation. The combination of these two processes tends to involve the harnessing of desire – again, like the war machine, a kind of resistance – by power, as a means of transforming and reinventing itself.

These processes and dynamics, however, don't just take place on the level of large epochal shifts, like the move from Fordism to post-Fordism. The approach developed by *Operaismo* and, in a slightly different way, Deleuze and Guattari, provides a more general way of thinking about the relation between power and resistance. We refer to a similar phenomenon, for example, when we talk about the development of summit protests and the counter-globalisation movement in *Move into the Light?* The discourse around poverty alleviation at the 2005 G8 Summit in Gleneagles, and climate change at Heiligendamm in 2007, illustrates, on the one hand, the power of our movements to move and set the global agenda. On the other, however, it demonstrates the means by which capital often seeks to harness movements of resistance – or the changes in public sentiment which they produces – and render them productive for itself.

At Gleneagles, a worldwide movement against global poverty and, more generally, for a better life than a constant struggle for bare survival, was translated into a discourse of poverty alleviation which eventually began to be deployed by the 'world leaders' themselves. By and large, it involved flirtation with the idea of a new global Keynesianism (what George Caffentzis has called neoliberalism's 'Plan B'). A billion people were to be lifted out of poverty through their fuller incorporation into the capitalist, wage-labouring economy. Whereas in the 1930s, Keynes saw a necessity for 'political' intervention into 'the economy' in order to create full employment (largely through the stimulation of demand) which he saw as the key to economic growth and stability, the global Keynesianism of 2005 involved considering similar interventions designed to turn large numbers of the 'global poor' into wage-labourers. The goal was to achieve full employment *par excellence* by turning those who reproduced themselves, at least in part, outside of capitalist social relations, into wage-labourers proper.

In Heiligendamm, we saw the heads of state recognise the pressing need to deal with the issue of climate change. In many ways, this was a victory for environmental campaigners and a relatively small number of climate change scientists who had been trying to highlight the issue for years. At the same time, it became increasingly clear as to how the challenge posed by climate change also offers a number of *possibilities* for capital. On the one hand, as we explain in *Move into the Light?*, this is likely to involve austerity measures: regressive 'green' taxation, restrictions on mobility and the consumption of 'luxuries', and so on. On the other, it is likely to mean the opening of new, potentially profitable, markets: carbon trading, climate consultancy, 'green' consumerism, etc.

The task with which struggles and resistance movements are confronted, then, is to remain aware of the way in which these processes operate. This is where the reasonably abstract ideas about power and resistance offered up by the *Operaisti* (as well as Deleuze and Guattari) has real, practical application. This recognition then provides a basis for both recognising our own agency; as well as the need to constantly rethink strategy, tactics, and the very nature of struggle as capital constantly develops new ways of imposing decomposition.

Michal Osterweil I want to raise a couple of related issues that I think often go unaddressed in leftist and movement discussions of strategy and social change: the role we play in creating the monster known as capitalism, and our insufficient attention to other problems, such as the dogmatisms and microfascisms, that sometimes arise precisely because of too rigid or too encompassing a theory or ideology.

As many people have already pointed out, a very serious problem on the Left is our complicity in creating a vision of capitalism as total, totalising and completely hegemonic. As J.K Gibson-Graham put it in *The End of Capitalism (As We Knew It)*, "the project of understanding the beast [capitalism] has itself produced a beast, or even a bestiary; and the process of producing knowledge in service to politics has estranged rather than united understanding and action." (There is an important difference here between ubiquity and totality. It is one thing to acknowledge that capitalism is everywhere (ubiquity), and quite another to speak of capitalism as having no outside and being that which defines all social relations (totality)).

While I have few qualms with the former, I believe that analyses based on the latter are very problematic in that they contribute to a sense of paralysis, powerlessness and hopelessness – leading so many of us to ask, 'What can we do that won't be co-opted or destroyed by capital?' However, they also obscure other issues and problems that are not necessarily reducible to capitalism's processes of accumulation, nor the antagonism between capital and labour. (Issues having to do with cultural and sexual difference, but also complicated issues of crime, gentrification, etc. come to mind.)

This is particularly interesting because it makes it difficult to know what action will really be most radical – most able to get at the heart of the system. For, while within the global justice movement we have been quick to distinguish between 'reformists' and 'radicals' – i.e. people with more systemic, or rather *anti*-systemic approaches, we neglect that the depiction of the system might create other obstacles to transformative change. For example, often, in our efforts to organise movements with an anti-systemic orientation – i.e. movements that understand that it is not just a matter of repealing a few misguided policies, or reforming institutions like the G8, World Bank, etc, but rather overturning or transforming an entire political, economic, cultural and social system – we not only make capital appear far more coherent and hegemonic than it actually is, we also make it seem like the definition of a more 'radical' approach is universal, or definable outside particular circumstances. Moreover, in the process we end up reproducing the kinds of movements and activist subjectivities that are unable to address and deal with complexities issues, and problems, which are not necessarily already explainable vis-à-vis the meta-analysis of capitalism those activists are working from.

The appeal of an anti-systemic analysis and vision of 'our enemy' always risks turning into a rigid, un-reflexive, and potentially problematic formula that people fall back on even in situations that are tremendously complicated. A very serious challenge at the core of the *Turbulence* project is finding ways to undermine the tendencies within so many of our movements (and ourselves!) to become so invested in one meta-narrative, ideology or reading of both the problem and the solution that we both help create the monster *and* neglect other issues and possibilities.

SL You make the point that we may not be able to recognise our victories, since some are not immediately visible. That's fair enough. It can be difficult to see which seeds will grow. But it's equally hard, or harder, to ask if we're failing. For example, opposition movements cannot necessarily take credit for the breakdown of multilateral negotiations within the World Trade Organisation, as these have been derailed, not by stateless movements, but specific nation-states. A contributor to *Turbulence* puts it in bold terms: the movement – or 'movement of movements' as you refer to it – is in crisis, following the mass mobilisation in Genoa in 2001. What do you think is the basis of that crisis?

BT This distinction between 'success' and 'failure' takes us back to the Morris quote mentioned earlier. What appears as a failure, in other words, often turns out to be some kind of a limited success. The challenge which then presents itself is moving beyond these limitations. And you're certainly right about identifying failures being as difficult as successes – and in a similar way. In other words, what initially appears as a *success* might, in some ways, also point towards certain *defeats*.

Let's take the example of the collapse of WTO negotiations, since you mentioned them. There have been at least three separate ministerials at which talks have either completely broken down (Seattle in 1999 and Cancún in 2003) or the agreement reached has been so precarious that it came undone almost immediately afterwards (Hong Kong in 2005). At each of these three events, despite enormous demonstrations and mass acts of disobedience, it was in fact a collection of state actors – largely acting in their own political and economic self-interest – which brought about the collapse of negotiations. So whilst movements celebrated this breakdown, and in part claimed the victory as their own, it would perhaps seem that it was states, or coalitions of states, which were able to derail negotiations and halt the neoliberal juggernaut, rather than 'stateless movements'. In this sense, the collapses could be interpreted as a sign of the agency of *constituted* over *constituent* forms of power.

There is certainly some truth to this. But the full reality is a little more complicated. There are, for instance, a number of ways in which the agency of movements can be seen as having influenced the behaviour of state actors within negotiations. First of all, there are powerful, popular anti-neoliberal movements in many of the countries which made up the G20 group of 'developing' nations, for instance, which played a key role in derailing the negotiation of the Doha Round in Cancún. The ability of these movements to influence domestic political and economic policy impacted on the position taken by state representatives engaging in international negotiations.

Secondly, the development of a worldwide movement against neoliberalism – which often took its cue from these movements in the South – as well as often spectacular scenes on the streets outside the summits themselves, almost certainly contributed to the legitimacy with which the G20 and other states were able to rupture negotiations.

There are certainly issues worth considering here as to where change does and does not take place, but there does seem to have been a (not-entirely deliberate) *working in concert* that took place between movements and state actors during the WTO negotiations. Precisely whether this represents a 'success' or 'failure' for movements, I'm not so sure. This is a question that The Free Association deal with at length in their article, 'Worlds in Motion', contained in this book.

In relation to the question of the counter-globalisation movement's crisis and its nature, I would agree that the current crisis began sometime around the mobilisation to Genoa in 2001. Although it is important to point out that what took place in Genoa was unlikely the sole, or even primary, cause of the crisis.

In terms of how this crisis can be understood, I think the movement – since 2001 – has undergone a number of *decompositions*. In other words, a reduction in its ability to act, intervene and influence has been experienced through a simultaneous attack on its forms of organisation (through the introduction of new legislation, transformations in policing, an escalation in the levels of violence generally waged against the movement), as well as significant changes in that which the movement is posited against: neoliberalism. This second aspect is connected to fall out from the flirtation with global Keynesianism by the G8 and others around 2005, mentioned above.

The conventional way of thinking of 'movements' – including by many people who consider themselves involved in them – is quite problematic. They are often thought of as discrete actors, with a clear inside and an out; generally possessing a 'consciousness' as to their own existence, as well as their aims and objectives. On one level, of course, movements do lead an existence on this level. Often, people either recognise themselves and/or others as 'belonging' to a movement, or not. There may be some quibbles – 'Those reformists have got nothing to do with us, we're a movement for real change.' 'The black bloc aren't part of our movement, we want a world without that sort of behaviour' – but this is often about relatively minor details.

The problem with this kind of a definition of movements, however, is that it privileges a particular kind of agency as the only – or primary – means by which change takes place. It's more useful, I think, to think of 'movement' occurring through the constant *moving* of social relations – i.e. the way in which we relate to one another and the means by which these relations are mediated.

Perhaps it's helpful to think about something like the counter-globalisation movement as constituting a *body* amongst a broader, permanent moving of relations within which it is embedded. In one of his books on Spinoza, Deleuze explains that the Dutch philosopher defined a body in two different, simultaneous ways. First of all, a body is something made up of an infinite number of 'particles', its individuality defined by the speed and slowness, motion and rest, between them. Secondly, it is defined by its capacity to affect (its power to act), which for Spinoza is always equal to its ability to be affected. A body undergoes a transformation, then, through changes in the way in which its (internal) particles move in relation to one another; as well as – relatedly – changes in its capacity to affect or be affected by other (external) bodies.

Applying this to the counter-globalisation movement, its body changes – and enters a crisis (in itself, not necessarily a bad or good thing) – through both altera-tions in the way in which its constituent parts act and relate to one another; as well as via a transformation in the way it behaves towards – or is treated by – other bodies. The fact that the borders between 'outside' and 'in' are, in the case of the counter-globalisation movement, so porous does not invalidate this understanding, but simply increase its complexity.

MO The conventional way of reading movements and their agency also tends to preclude recognising the multiple levels or scales at which movements move and act. In fact, one could argue that one of the most important 'outcomes' of movement can be seen at more micro-political or cultural levels including the production or cultivation of different kinds of subjectivities; subjectivities that are willing to put their assumptions, practices, political analyses into question. In this sense while it is certainly hard to know or ask about whether a movement is failing, the clearest sign of the failure of movement is when the movement becomes a static category or space, with rigid boundaries and fixed content, where actors within it participate and proceed uncritically.

It is quite refreshing to see how many people are in a place of questioning, reflec-tion, and research, not only for effective ways of opposing capitalism, the G8, etc. but of how to organize our lives differently. I recognize that this might sound like I am romanticizing the idea of uncertainty, but I don't think it has to be that way. There is a difference between the type of uncertainty that leads to inaction or paralysis and the kind that I think is evidenced by people's interest in *Turbulence*. That is people that want to act, do, move, but recognize and are open to the fact that they might not already know the exact way forward. I think this is particularly important especially when we consider the rather violent, polemical political culture that surrounds us – both more mainstream electoral politics, but also within so-called progressive spaces, or the left more generally. A political culture where one is constantly compelled to fight for the truth or superiority of one's position, rather than recognize the messy, contingent nature of all political work.

SL Your argument that the crisis of the global justice movement(s) can be traced to repression on the one hand and shifts in the nature of neoliberalism on the other seems incomplete at best. In the spirit of not proceeding uncritically, one would have to point out that such an argument lets these movements themselves – however we might conceptualise their form – off the hook. And it sidesteps the many legitimate questions that have been raised about the strategies and goals of the movements, including most immediately whether protesting at summits makes sense either for

movement-building or for framing opposition to the capitalist system. So what of the movements themselves? How have strategic and political choices, conscious or not, fed into this impasse?

MO I do not think we have claimed that the 'crisis' or impasse of the counter-globalisation movement has to do *only* with repression or shifts in the nature of neoliberalism, nor have we denied that the agency and choices of movement actors are themselves worth critiquing, analysing, and reviewing. On the contrary, our project is premised on the belief that we need more spaces in which to critically and honestly assess the effectiveness of activist and movement practices, as well as their strategies and visions. But we believe that the criteria by which effectiveness, or even what counts as movement, are judged also need to be critically assessed. Constructively analysing impasses on the one hand, and movement successes on the other, requires complicating our views of both politics and social change. Often substantial change does not only include things we typically look for in measuring political outcomes – e.g., legislative change, building large movement organisations, actually shutting down a multilateral institution. Change also happens at more subtle levels, acting as a potential, creating the conditions of possibility for *other* futures, emergences.

I think most of us would agree that, for all their weaknesses, counter-summit protests have been productive and successful in many ways, even if they have not eliminated the supposed 'targets' of their protest. Besides eroding the hegemony and claims to legitimacy of many of the multinational institutions that enforce neoliberalism – including the G8, WTO, IMF, and the World Bank – these counter-summits have been very important in terms of cultivating radically different subjectivities, with radically different visions of how social life can and should be. These transnational protests create spaces in which other ways of being and organising life can be attempted and experimented. So, rather than judge counter-summits negatively, in terms of whether they disrupt or eliminate transnational institutions, we must be able to evaluate them in terms of what they produce and generate. Politically vital in and of themselves, these include high levels of energy and affect, experiences in collaboration, as well as the immense villages and events that get constructed around them. Rather than judge the movements as failures because they did not fully shut down the institutions, or curtail neoliberalism, we must understand that the successes of counter-summits are difficult to measure, or even see, given our current categories and vocabularies, because they exist at these 'other' levels.

That said, I would agree that those of us – especially those of us in the global North – seeking to make movement have not been very effective at building sustainable, durable spaces and structures outside the exceptional times and spaces of counter-summits, social forums, etc. Nor have we been very good at recognising that a key level of the success of the global social justice movement has to do with this other level of politics; a level that involves not only the macro defeat of neoliberal institutions and policies but the production and refining of diverse knowledges and capacities. In this sense, it is not that counter-summit protests and other mass events were ill-advised or bad strategies, but once again, we have not carried the lessons and strong points of those moments through to their logical developments. In other words, we need to figure out how to articulate the new ideas, experiences and practices born at the height of these exceptional moments, more durably to daily life and for a much wider public.

SL Like the movements celebrated in this book, a significant part of the New Left also emphasised decentralisation and localism, symbolic protest, direct action, the empowerment of those who had been marginalised, as well as a commitment to rejecting the mistakes of the traditional Left. Yet many of these attributes are now being championed as unique to current movements for global justice. If "illumination" is a concern – the question of what can and can't be perceived – shouldn't an effort be made to place these movements in historical context? And isn't there real risk, when one is close to, or a participant in, a movement, that one's assessment may be distorted by proximity?

BT The issue of proximity is an important one. None of the editors want *Turbulence* to become a project in which our own involvement with the movements addressed leads us to becoming so caught up in 'internal' movement debates that we lose sight of broader dynamics; or, equally disastrous, that we end up overestimating the (currently rather limited) social relevance of that which is often called the 'movement of movements'.

I think Lenin's writing on the function of political newspapers are relevant here. In a text called *Where to Begin?* Lenin argued that newspapers do not just serve the function of propaganda and agitation, but also organisation. "In this last respect", he said, "it may be likened to the scaffolding round a building under construction, which marks the contours of the structure and facilitates communication between builders, enabling them to distribute the work and to view the common results achieved by their organised labour."

I think this scaffolding metaphor is helpful. Both the form and the pace of its construction, in order to be of use, needs to be determined by the real productive process of movement building. If it begins moving too rapidly away from that which it is designed to aid in the construction of, it becomes redundant. At the same time however, a certain amount of distance can also open up space for expansion or development in unforeseen directions. The fact that we do not know what the final construction – the movement – will look like means the scaffolding requires a far greater degree of flexibility than if it were simply to aid something clearly designed by a single architect, following a tried and tested blueprint.

Obviously, it is not only newspapers or other publishing projects that serve this function. Social forums, conferences, and other gatherings can also enable a similar process of collective reflection on, and distribution of work within, a process of organisation. We would very much like to think that *Turbulence* could become one part of this movement scaffolding; and we hope that we will be able to judge these

WHAT WOULD IT MEAN TO WIN?

questions of proximity and distance appropriately, although I'm sure we've made plenty of mistakes in this respect already!

I think the issue of repetition is also really interesting. In the opening few pages of *The Eighteenth Brumaire*, Marx describes the way in which revolutionary uprisings or events often invoke past occurrences. He compares this process to learning a language, where a beginner always starts by translating back into her first language. Yet it is only when the mother tongue can be forsaken, and this process of translation left behind, that one can properly enter into the spirit of the new language and start speaking it with fluency. So while it is true that on the one hand, "Tradition from all the dead generations weighs like a nightmare on the brain of the living"; on the other, there is sometimes something enabling and productive in this process of repetition.

I would like to think that much of the (only partial) repetition of the New Left which has characterised the counter-globalisation movement has mostly taken place in this sense. Language of difference, autonomy, opposition to authoritarianism, and the rejection of hierarchy were all characteristics of the movements of the 1960s and 1970s – in the global North at least. And all have been redeployed by the 'movement of movements'. But I think this has largely involved a process of renewal, rather than parody. And as others have argued much more fully elsewhere, changes in the mode of production and regulation, as well as new technological developments, have enabled this process of horizontalisation and the formation of more genuinely-networked networks (like the 'rhizomes' described at the beginning of Deleuze and Guattari's *A Thousand Plateaus*, characterised by de-centredness and many-to-many connections – whilst always *also* still containing centralising or hierarchical elements within them) to go much further than was the case with the New Left.

By and large, this has been a great thing. The problem arises, however, when this returns to being ideology, as was the case with parts of the movements of the '60s and '70s. Certainly, there is a huge amount to be learned from the problems generated by what could be called the 'undemocratic' movement practices of yesteryear (where democracy is understood as the ability of everyone to fully participate in the constitution of society). But ideological opposition to experimentation with, for example, 'mass' forms of political organisation that tend to involve some form of delegation and representation; or cooperation with 'non-autonomous' social actors, such as trade unions or political parties, on the basis of maintaining difference/identity/'autonomy' can be tremendously debilitating.

Rather than defending identities *per se*, surely the idea ought to become creating forms and practices where difference no longer provides the basis for establishing hierarchies of privilege. And to be sure, there are strong tendencies within the 'movement of movements' in this direction of identitarianism. But my feeling is that these stand for a politics that already, long ago, ran up against its limits. I feel that there's an increasing recognition of this. There seems to be a new pragmatics infused with the knowledge, experience and sometimes 'ethics' of past movements; but nevertheless with a greater openness towards experimentation with organisational forms, the building of transversal connections between micropolitical struggles, and a larger emphasis on *becoming* over being than was often the case with the New Left.

MO This question seems to have multiple levels of concern: on the one hand there appears to be a simple factual or empirical question. Just how '*new*' are the logics, visions and effects discussed at length in this book, and often associated with the post-Seattle movements for global justice, really? But, on the other, this question itself has to do with assumptions about the nature of history and progress, as well as what the relationship between knowledge and social change is or should be.

I have actually been quite struck by how concerned people seem to be about whether or not it is true that the movements for global justice offer unique or new political insights and approaches. However, rather than concerning myself with answering that question directly, I have become quite interested in why people ask it. What is at stake? I suppose at one level it seems obvious: clearly one wants to be as accurate as possible. After all, we live in a society where competitions over truth-claims seem to posit the difference between accepting reality or denying it (just think about the 'scientific debates' on global climate change, for instance.) But at another level it might be interesting to step back for a moment and ask why. Why does it matter if the 'movement of movements' is new or different from past movements, like those that emerged in the late 1960s and are associated with the New Left? What assumptions, fears or anxieties underlie the concern about whether the claim to uniqueness is false? What would it mean if the qualities being lauded were *not* new or unique? What happens if they are actually repetitions?

I want to suggest that if we start thinking seriously about these questions we can begin to see that underlying the seemingly obvious or neutral curiosity about the accuracy of claims to novelty, are rather strong normative positions about the nature of history, progress and reality itself. These positions and rationalities not only shape possible interpretations, they also make or obscure other ways of doing politics.

One interpretation that would understandably lead to concern is one based on the idea that these movements are simply repeating past mistakes. That is the New Left's vision or theory of social change that emphasised decentralisation, localism, micropolitics, etc. was wrong then; and using a correspondence model of history, movements must be wrong now. This interpretation also presumes that it is because of an error inherent to their political analysis that the New Left failed. (The error itself could have been caused by a number of things, for example the Left misread or misunderstood the real nature of what they were against, the particularities of the conjuncture, etc.) I think this belief is the source of much of the anxiety about just how new the 'movement of movements' really is. However, I would also suggest that not too far beneath the surface of these worries lies a particular normative view that treats history as progressive, linear, and often working like a zero-sum game. In this way of viewing things, *knowing* whether these movements are the same or similar to those in the past, is important because repetition means lack of progress.

Or, at the very best, it indicates an inability to learn from past failures. In either case the implication is that 'really knowing' our history – in this case, recognising that these practices are at least to some extent *not* new – should convince us that there is really nothing to be gained from (re)investing in the approach. After all, these practices were already proven to be failures. And moreover that any excitement and hope surrounding these positive beliefs actually distracts us from the *real work* of inventing politics that would actually count as new. This I would argue is quite a pervasive view, and helps us understand why so many people are concerned with whether or not there is something new here.

But what if it was not the fact that the analyses and practices of the New Left were wrong, but that they were never taken far enough? What if the guiding theories, visions, and implicit strategies etc were right, but that for a number of reasons the New Left never achieved success? We know that even according to its own analyses, true success would require complete transformation of the cultural, epistemological and ontological foundations of the then present. In other words, the changes required were so radical and thorough that even activists and others who believed in over-turning the capitalist system – which they viewed as much more than an economic system – were unable to go far enough. (Whether that was because they didn't have enough time, they were themselves too deeply entrenched in the dominant culture, or the political and economic Right were effective in interfering, is an important question but not necessary to answer here.)

SL I would disagree that placing movements in historical perspective leads one down the slippery path to a positivist notion of 'progress'. Attempting to get a handle on history, including the history of prior struggles, debates, successes and failures, has great value. It allows us to resurrect tools from the past to arm ourselves in the present, to take a hard look at where the Left may be repeating its mistakes, to think strategically while taking a long view, and even to ask some of the questions that you are posing above.

I raised the question of 'originality' because I've been intrigued by the frequency of claims by participants that these movements are unique and have broken with the earlier modus operandi of the Left (including in your piece '"Becoming-Woman?" In Theory or Practice' where you write that current movements embody and posit 'deliberate reactions to the practical and theoretical failures of previous political approaches of the Left.') The reality strikes me as something quite different – that there is, in fact, much more continuity than rupture. The question I would counterpose is that, given this, why are today's movements so invested in seeming new? What's at stake for them?

MO To begin with, I want to stress that I do not at all dismiss the importance of learning from history. In fact, the argument I am making, both in this interview and in 'Becoming-Woman?', is premised on the importance of historical knowledge, interest, and interrogation. Claims to uniqueness, novelty, and rupture by no means negate historical trajectories and lineages; they are in fact premised on them. In fact, while one might assume that narratives of continuity and rupture are opposed, I want to suggest that they are mutually constitutive and dependent on each other. For it is only with historical knowledge and understanding that we can begin to claim that our *current* politics are attempts to address the failures of *past* politics. In other words, the very argument that our current political movements are deliberately enacting forms of politics and movement meant to address the pitfalls of old models, suggests that we know and seek to understand what those past politics were and why they failed. Whether our understandings of what those past failures were is accurate is another question altogether, but I want to be clear that I in no way refute the importance of placing movements in historical context, nor assume that all attempts at putting movements in historical context are necessarily premised on positivist notions of progress.

That said, I do wonder whether, underlying this question about newness and originality, there weren't also certain conscious or unconscious positivist and/or historicist assumptions and anxieties at play. In general I think many of us on the 'Left' are plagued by a certain latent historicism, the sense that if we could just get it right, ultimately we will achieve victory against capitalism. (Borrowing from Derrida, I could suggest that this is perhaps one of Marx's many spectres that continues to haunt us and our visions of social change.)

I return to my earlier response: There is a difference in the assumption that the New Left failed because its theories and political ideals – i.e. horizontalism, anti-hierarchy, localism, etc. – were themselves inherently flawed, and a view that argues that the theories guiding the New Left were not taken far enough.

Here it is critical to see that the political analysis that accompanies commitment to localism, decentralisation, horizontality, etc. is itself based on a recognition that beyond the macro-institutional and economic systems, culture and micro-politics form the terrain where hegemonies of the current economic and political regimes maintain themselves. This means that the dominance of these systems are both manifested in and dependent upon various cultural elements, including subjectivity, social institutions and social relations, the unspoken rules that govern the micro-practices of daily life; as well as cultural logics such as progress, individualism, and identity. As such, successful strategies of resistance must confront not only the political-institutional and economic manifestations of neoliberal capitalist globalisation, but also, and at the same time, the foundational cultural logics and the everyday practices and social relations that both constitute, produce, and make the dominance of these systems possible. This is especially important because these logics and practices all too often manifest themselves among organisations that call themselves progressive – including many movement organisations, and certainly the traditional Left. The conception of history as linear and progressive, as well as the notion that there is one certain path to revolution, are both examples of how these logics persist.

As such, to engage in effective struggle requires radically challenging not only a current economic or political system; but enacting, sustaining and cultivating other ways of being. But rethinking and remaking the ways we are and do in the world is a tremendous task, one that requires a great deal of time and space for elaborating, experimenting and even failing at times. Rather than dismiss the apparent repetitions as products of historical ignorance, it might be more helpful to see them as attempts to take these practices farther, aware of the limitations of past attempts, but optimistic about the possibilities that trying again, *differently*, might bring.

The important point is to recognise that there is a fundamental difference here between a perspective that sees the repetition of many things that characterised the New Left as evidence of ignorance and naïveté, and a likely indicator of current movements' meagre prospects; and another approach that sees the repetition as a *possibility for more thorough follow-through* – 'renewing' as Ben says. This renewal is itself based on critically engaging with earlier attempts, but also builds on the innovations and changes brought about by technological advances and global connectedness, on the one hand, but also by the lessons, cultural practices and ideals and more intensive engagements with the legacies of the 1960s and the New Left, on the other – including in particular, more intensive understandings of the meaning and value of radical ontological difference, and the partiality of any view or subject position.

I have always found the temporal politics of judging movements quite perplexing: we are talking on the one hand about a system and culture – 'Western Capitalist Modernity' – that has been violently and systemically fought for, produced, defended, and entrenched for several centuries, and yet we expect 'movements' to somehow be able to successfully overthrow that system (of which we are all largely products) and remake society anew in a matter of a few years or decades? That expectation seems unrealistic and indeed part of the problem.

Claiming newness and rupture, then, is not necessarily about false consciousness or denying history but potentially the most natural and hopeful claim someone can make. Again, newness does not mean rejecting everything from the past. It means rearticulating it. It also suggests recognising that the past (even the past of the Left) is dense and multiple.

There's a beautiful Zapatista quote that is relevant here: "We will walk then the same path of history, but we will not repeat it; we are from before, yes, but we are new." Not only have the Zapatistas inspired many all over the world with their understanding of the need for a humble and reflexive approach that changes while it unfolds, they are themselves the products of profound clashes between radically different subjects who challenge simplistic divisions between 'old' and 'new': e.g. clashes between urban guerrillas who tried to bring Marxist visions of social change to indigenous communities, only to find that rather than convince the indigenous that they held the recipe for revolution, they were themselves transformed by learning that indigenous communities had their own systems of knowledge and politics, many that were profoundly more democratic and sustainable. Inherent in

147

the Zapatista valorisation and use of history, then, is precisely this double-movement: a recognition of their connection to diverse pasts, diverse revolutionary efforts; part of a long, enduring path, with tumultuous curves and twists, and the continuous and inevitable production of new realities along this path that gives one the possibility and necessity of being new. In this way of seeing things, repetition is not a real risk or possibility, because the subjects walking the path are necessarily constituted by all the sediment, cultural, technological and otherwise left behind, on the hand, and by the difference of the present: the possibility of *this time*, *this place*, *maybe*, getting it right – or at least doing it better. (For as some philosophers and the Zapatistas remind us, what we call repetition can only exist with the constitutive and generative presence of difference.)

SL Most of these essays assume that the common ground between these numerous movements is opposition to capitalism. But is that a fair assumption? Many people in these movements take to the streets against the market, neoliberalism, or against corporations, but that doesn't necessarily mean they oppose capitalism as a system.
MO Certainly, I agree. Not everyone who has participated in the movements against the World Bank, G8, NAFTA, etc. would identify themselves as anti-capitalist, nor would they perhaps agree with our calling them that. But I guess to that I would say that the term itself doesn't matter all that much. (And I might even be convinced – though I think other editors might disagree – that perhaps we need to find a better word, one that is not so loaded historically and theoretically for people.) I would argue that even those working with a rather limited (reformist) agenda, seeking to curb the power of the G8 and other institutional sites of corporate driven neoliberal globalisation without undoing capitalism completely, have also been inspired, energised and motivated at least in part by the anti-systemic nature and effects of the 'new' politics of the 'movement of movements' – whether they recognise it or not. In other words the qualities that excite people – the network form, the diversity, the affect (all part of a minoritarian political modality) that so many people from various political stripes speak so much about – resonate and work precisely because they hit against, and between, something that is far bigger and more systemic than the specific economic policies of the WTO, IMF or multinational corporations. They hit against an entire culture of politics, and at the same time, they reveal the cultural foundations of the political and economic institutions they are seeking to reform.

It is only when we consider the political analysis accompanying commitments to decentralisation, horizontality, localism that we can begin to understand that those things that make people identify with the 'movement of movements,' have everything to do with their discovering a different cultural-political modality. A cultural-political modality that becomes visible as it reveals and discovers sites and possibilities for disrupting the present, a present that is decidedly and systemically capitalist. Again, we could also call the system something else. The point is recognising that there is an entire system and culture, not simply a set of bad economic policies or institutions that we are struggling against. And the fact is even if we don't use the label, we discover this when victories, or the 'affect of winning', accompanies events and things that don't neatly translate into traditional ways of measuring political outcomes.

In addition, part of what was so powerful about social movements' experiences in recent years was – rather than proceed according to a map or plan for social change, whether that was defined as defeating capitalism, or simply demanding certain reforms – the ways in which working with such a diversity of actors and experiences brought in the unexpected. Such that it was not only, or even primarily, the contents of our movements, but also our very form, that could, often unexpectedly, both create (new) cracks and reveal myriad existing gaps and holes in the dominant (capitalist) system. A system that is as much dependent on people thinking that there is only one way of being and doing – economics, community, social relations – and that certain human characteristics are both natural and inevitable, rather than a product of this system, as it is in accumulating profits.

So to reiterate: although I agree that many people are committed to very pragmatic, 'achievable,' or reformist goals against neoliberalism and the economic hegemons of today, and do not subscribe to the *label* of anti-capitalist, this does not mean that their political effectiveness does not register at a more systemic level – whether we call it anti-capitalist or something else.

BT OK, in answering this question, let me take a very quick detour through Marx's critique of capitalism – what he called his critique of political economy – and how it applies to the way we live and work today, before trying to explain what this has to do with the political practice of the counter-globalisation movement or the global Left.

Personally, I think it is more useful to think not about 'capital-ism' as a *system*, but about 'capital' as a *social relation*. Most of us, today, live in a situation in which we are denied access to the means of our own reproduction: food, shelter, clothing, the latest iPhone, whatever. Our bare survival and everything else, in other words, is premised on selling our time on the market in return for a wage. Of course, in some places, a welfare state still exists. But this increasingly serves, on the one hand, as a cushion to absorb frustrations likely to lead us to rebel rather than starve; and on the other, to provide some kind of a 'post-industrial' reserve army that allows average wages to be kept low.

In the process of selling our time, we do not only generate enough 'wealth' to cover that received in our wages, but also a surplus which is appropriated. 'Capital' is the name of both this relation of exploitation, as well as one pole within it. Once locked inside this relation, there is a constant attempt on behalf of capital to increase the surplus extracted. This happens through increasing the length of the average working day: cutting back on holiday periods, reducing the length of breaks, getting people to stay late or come in early, requiring work at the weekend, encouraging workers to take their work home with them, etc. This is what Marx describes as the process of 'absolute surplus value extraction'. At the same time, capital tries to increase efficiency: introducing new technologies, rearranging the labour-process, imposing discipline through surveillance, encouraging self-discipline by increasing workers' control over the productive process (as was the case, for example, at Toyota). Translated into Marxian: this is, very broadly speaking, 'relative surplus value extraction'.

Individual capitalists, of course, might be more or less philanthropic. Or more or less innovative in extending or intensifying periods of worker exploitation. But taken at a total social level, there is a constantly waged class struggle from above geared towards increasing absolute and relative surplus extraction. The only limits to this are, on the one hand, natural (the working day obviously cannot be extended beyond 24 hours, and at some point a worker would simply drop dead), and on the other, determined by class struggle from below.

Again, struggles against the extension of the working day (or for its shortening), or against the introduction of new technologies or the restructuring of the labour process, have been far more intensive in some regions, periods and industries than others. But taken as a whole, all these struggles play an extremely important role in determining the rate of exploitation.

Looked at in this way, it is not *only* those of us consciously involved with the counter-globalisation movement whose everyday lives are embedded in these relations of antagonism, but the vast majority of humanity. Simply living today – whether that is understood as bare survival, or struggling for a better existence – implies resistance to capital's never ending efforts to intensify exploitation. A very large part of the 'movement of movements' in the global North has tended to focus on this process of exploitation as it manifests itself in its most extreme form, such as sweatshops in parts of the global South. Likewise, it has often addressed the commodification of nature and the ecological crises this is generating; as well as conflicts over resources, such as oil. For me, this means that the movement is anti-capitalist whether or not it describes itself as such. It takes on the very logic described above, as well as many of its by-products (enclosure and war, for example). I don't think that there is really any necessity for the movement to always call itself 'anti-capitalist', and some of the alternatives it proposes of course do not break entirely with capital's logic, but it is important to recognise what it is that the movement is in conflict with.

What should be pointed out, however, is the extent to which the movement in the global North – including those parts which *do* explicitly regard themselves as anti-capitalist or 'revolutionary' – fails to translate this into a political practice directed towards their own involvement in processes of social production and reproduction.

SL On the other hand, by defining resistance to capitalism so broadly, one might conclude that there is no reason to build movements, think strategically, or even figure out how to win people over to an anti-capitalist outlook – since through the labour process, we're all effectively involved in resisting capitalism. And the claim

that it isn't really important if people identify capitalism as the ultimate enemy raises similar concerns. There is nothing intrinsically anti-capitalist about opposition to 'globalisation', itself a tremendously murky term, which for radicals may mean the expansion of capital on a global scale, but for others may mean the contamination of supposedly pristine national cultures by undesirable foreigners. Shouldn't the fact that much of the Right is against 'globalisation' give us pause in assuming that a simply oppositional stance will lead people to taking on the system of capitalism, rather than pursuing potential red herrings like defending 'national sovereignty'?

BT There are at least two separate issues at stake here. First of all, you are of course correct that there are a number of serious dangers involved with pursuing a politics of 'anti-globalisation'. The Right, around the world, have generally been critical of what they regard as the erosion of national identities and sovereignty; something the Left, or the radical Left at least, would tend to celebrate. Much of the global movement, however, has been fairly clear that its opposition is far more to a particular kind of *neoliberal* globalisation, than to the opening of borders to movement, communication and hybridisation in general. It is a movement founded in opposition to the reality it emerges from, but whose practices and discourses – albeit somewhat incoherently – *propose a different kind of globalisation*. Of course, with the attempt to repeat earlier European imperialist projects during the era of the Bush administration, much of the Left returned to a language of anti-imperialism. This was often rooted in an uncritical relationship to the notions of 'the nation', 'sovereignty' and so on. The failure of these so-called 'new imperialist' projects, in both Iraq and Afghanistan, will likely also present a problem for 'anti-imperialism' – where 'critical' solidarity tends to be expressed with anyone resisting the projection of a nation state's sovereignty beyond its own borders. As more multilateral efforts are sought to impose a particular kind of stability in those regions, I imagine the global Left will begin rethinking the way in which a resurgent Empire can be resisted.

The other issue you raise, about whether we should be attempting to win people over to an anti-capitalist outlook, I understand as addressed to the questions of consciousness, spontaneity and organisation. These are difficult questions which were dealt with extensively by the workers' movement at the beginning of the last century and which still have not been resolved. To be sure, I believe there is an important role for organization. Moreover, I believe that we have yet to discover organisational forms capable of adequately dealing with the changed composition of the working class brought about by the uneven but definite move from the era of Fordism/Keynesianism to post-Fordism/neoliberalism – let alone the as yet to be determined mutations the current epoch is about to go through as a result of the current economic crisis. For the Left, the project of experimenting with and developing new organisational forms is, then, one of the most important with which it is confronted.

At the same time, what our text, *Move into the Light?*, is all about is trying to recognise that movements do not always emerge where we expect, or take forms or use a language which those of us on the Left necessarily immediately recognise in their radicality. It is precisely the fact that struggles sometimes emerge where they are least expected which poses the biggest challenge to the development of organizational forms. The task is to try and create modes of institutionalising movements into sustainable forms of counter-power, but where this institutionalisation does not imply sedentarism. We need institutions which can move, because the world never really stands still.

SL It's certainly fair to criticise the Left's past dogmatic approach – what you call the 'old-school politics of certainty' – but it appears that these movements have swung to the opposite end of the spectrum. That leaves one with a very nebulous sense of what unifies them, aside from a limited opposition to the free market. And isn't there a danger in celebrating fragmentation and fluidity of organisation, when these characteristics may signal the weakness of these movements and the lack of unity between them? Just as we may be blind to our successes, might we mistakenly see our limitations as strengths?

MO I think that this is a very important question, and one that we do need to devote serious energy to – but I don't see it so much as a problem of positing and celebrating fragmented and fluid organisation against unity. Rather it is a matter of finding ways of imagining forms of unity that also allow for difference, flexibility, and dispersion. I say this because not only would I suggest that these would be more durable and effective versions of unity, they also run less risk of reproducing the forms of problematic social relations discussed in previous questions. At the same time it is also a matter of recognising that part of the ethic in which fluidity and fragmentation might be celebrated, has corollary principles including partiality, reflexivity, and contingency. As such we can only take these seriously if we do not turn fluidity and fragmentation into hard and fast ideologies or 'rules for good movements,' that would then not be open to the particularity and specificity of different circumstances and contexts.

This is largely a matter of perspective, and we might ask, what is at stake in claiming unity on the one hand, versus fluidity/fragmentation on the other? I would suggest that generally the concern that drives people to want more unity, and less fragmentation is the feeling or belief that in order to be effective we need to create such a powerful opposition that we are able to defeat the enemy or force it to make concessions. And moreover, that part of why we haven't been effective is that we can never put all our energies together to exert enough power against capitalism to defeat it, and then in Negri and Hardt's words, "push through ...to come out the other side."

However I would argue that fluid, diverse and disperse struggles can cumulatively exert forces that are potentially even more powerful. Not only by opposing capitalism, but by revealing and discovering cracks and holes that are already here (often as a result of prior oppositions), cracks that we can push open and connect. The effect of this might be to lessen capital's strength not simply by taking it down battle style, but by proliferating so many other ways of being that capitalism is no longer as central, necessary and powerful in determining the order of things, or at least how people perceive the order of things.

Here we might consider the distinction between ubiquity and totality, and the corollary visions of social change that accompany them. There is a huge difference between imagining a movement that manages to be everywhere, even if differently, and a unified mass movement that clearly comes from somewhere and whose inside is easily delimitable from its outside. As Gibson-Graham and others have pointed out, feminism is an excellent example of the former: an effective and transformative movement that worked less by building massive united organisations and alliances, and more through generating cultural consciousness, tools and ethics that spread virally and differently, ultimately including many people over vast geographies without ever fitting the description of a unity.

The common denominator, whether recognised by everyone in this way or not is that in the common experiences of opposition to a current way of organising the present, people have discovered different things, but underlying those different things is the common idea and possibility that other forms of politics, other ways of being, are possible, and already being co-created. You are right, though, we definitely need to spend more time discussing, discovering and articulating these because there is a tremendous strength gained by seeing how our different projects, strategies, and tools work together, even when not fully coordinated. It makes you recognise that things can and do work, and are not simply symbolic. But again, we need to articulate them not as if we are looking to establish new blueprints or road maps. We need to be able to share our stories, ideas, and narratives so that we can tease out commonalities, and even perhaps give us a better insight into what does work and doesn't without creating new dogmatisms.

BT I would answer both 'yes' and 'no' to both these questions. *No*, because I think it is useful to *begin* with a negative definition of the movement: not *for* a particular kind of socialism, for example; but first and foremost, *against* capitalism, or the free market, or whatever.

But yes, you are right, this is not enough. This negative moment can only be the very beginning. If we say 'Another World Is Possible', which of course it is, it seems ridiculous to fail or refuse to talk about what that world would or could look like. I tried to address this question in the article, 'Walking in the Right Direction?', included in this book. I talked about the (albeit often limited) role that demands have played in previous movements as well as current experiments with so-called 'directional demands'. To briefly summarise, I proposed the articulation of demands which fulfill certain criteria. Firstly, their realisation – either individually, or when taken together – should necessitate a break with capitalist social relations. Secondly, they should aim towards constituting commonalities amongst a vast multiplicity of social subjects, rather than privileging one (like the male industrial worker, for example). Thirdly, there should be no single point, or limit on the number of points, from which demands can be articulated; rather this articulation should take place through the movement of antagonistic social subjects. Finally, the demands should not follow a logic of linear accumulation, or traditional notions of 'progress' or 'development'; but rather should have as their aim a 'deterritorialisation' which opens things up for new possibilities and potentialities.

The two examples I cited of possible directional demands, going some way towards fulfilling these criteria, were 'a universal basic income', and something like 'freedom of movement' and/or 'the right to remain/legalisation'. On the one level, both contain the potential to create rupture within capitalist social relations. A guaranteed income, delinked from productivity requirements, undermines one of the fundamental characteristics of capitalism: the requirement to sell one's labour-power in order to survive (unless of course one owns considerable property!) And an undoing of mechanisms of migration management would also pose an enormous challenge to a global regime of accumulation based on the attribution of different economic values to labour performed in different locations.

Equally important, however, is the fact that these demands – or perhaps general 'desires', like for the reappropriation of the social wealth we produce, or to move freely – *already exist*. What I was not proposing is to come up with a renewal of Lenin's famous formulation: electrification + soviets = communism (something perhaps like: reappropriation + global citizenship = what ever it is that we say instead of 'communism' today). I don't believe in these kind of magic formulas. What I think we need to do, though, is both think about the ways in which those of us involved with social movements can start using a language which does not sound antiquated, and which explains what we want in a way that seeks to find resonance (rather than simply reproduce identity, as is so often the case with a lot of what the Left says and does). Equally important is to start listening more closely to the demands, desires and ideas of others. We need to start training ourselves to recognise the radicality in a lot of what people say and do which often go unnoticed because it does not pass as the usual way of doing or talking 'politics' (whatever that is!)

Fragmentation is certainly nothing to celebrate (although you are right, it very often is). And 'unity' is not really something I think we should be striving for. At least, not in the way it has generally been conceived philosophically, or in terms of its previous deployment by the 'traditional' Left. Michal mentioned Hardt and Negri, and I think that their work on the notion of 'multitude' is useful in this respect, particularly in the way it builds on the Spinozian rejection of a binary opposition between the 'One' and the 'many'.

For me, the placing of primacy on the agency of the male, industrial worker by traditional Marxist-Leninism involved a problematic sublimation of difference in the name of unity. Involved with this process was not only a serious limit on the extent to which the workers' movements could articulate both the needs and the desires of the range of social subjects in whose interests it claimed to be acting; but also a serious obscuration of important terrains of anti-capitalist struggle outside

the direct realm of industrial production. However, the polar opposite of this position – a blind faith in 'spontaneism', a retreat to identity politics, a total rejection of
everything that seeks to pursue change on the level of macropolitics – is, albeit in
very different ways, equally unsatisfactory.

What Hardt and Negri, and others like Paolo Virno, have tried to do with the
concept of multitude is to think a social subject which is internally heterogeneous,
yet nevertheless manages to constitute a coherent social actor. 'Unity' is not really
the goal; but rather to uncover and create *commonalities* amongst a vast multiplicity
of singularities. Whether or not people choose to work with the term, I think this
notion of multitude is very helpful when considering this question of organisation.

**SL You describe how movements can coalesce around opposition to something, as
happened in Seattle, Genoa, Cancún and Heiligendamm, and these moments can lead
from the strictly oppositional to advocating a positive agenda. But beyond potentially
improved strategy and tactics, what shared ideas are coming out of these gatherings?**
BT These movements were, first and foremost, oppositional movements. The nuns
and queers, environmentalists and trade unionists, anarchists and communists
who took to the streets of Seattle – and the similarly contradictory constellations of
actors which have since appeared in Genoa, Cancún and Heiligendamm, to pick up
on the examples you cite – at first glance, do not have that much in common. Their
immediate interests and stated objectives appear at odds with one another. Yet they
were nevertheless able to discover something that they had in common: a shared
opposition to the present.

And in many ways, I think it is a helpful way for movements to define themselves.
As John Holloway has argued much more powerfully elsewhere, movements' negative self-definition often allows them to avoid falling into sectarian discussions and
debates about how, precisely, the world would – or could – be remade in the future. It
enables communists, anarchists, socialists, radical-ecologists and others to establish
a common – negative – struggle: *against capitalism*. And in and through developing
this common struggle, new ways of relating, being and becoming end up coming
about anyway. And it is these practices which open room for new, shared ideas.

MO I see the fact of these collective discoveries that Ben mentions – the discoveries
of new ways of relating, being, etc. – as an important part of what might be called
a common-sense that has emerged out of recent movements. It is no coincidence
that so many of the most repeated and resonant terms to emerge from the global
mobilisations – including the Zapatista '*caminar preguntando*' (to walk while questioning), the notion of 'open space' and encounter – point to a way of creating the
ideas and theories of our movements in a very ongoing and reflexive way. As such
it is not a matter of finding a way of defining the ideas, objectives and visions of the
movement and then using that definition as a blue-print, or map; but rather discovering a new way of producing theories and analysis in ways that are more attentive to

contingency, particularity, etc. The fact that so many ideas have been 'discovered' in and through political events, rather than out of more abstract or intellectual efforts, is a testament to the fact that *how* and where ideas and theories gets produced, has everything to do with how effective they will be.

SL This interview is being conducted while the capitalist financial system is in freefall. It may be too early to tell, but it appears as if neoliberalism is in serious trouble and a more overtly interventionist state – or rather, a more *visibly* interventionistic state, since a *laissez-faire* system is dependent on massive state involvement to undergird markets and protect private property – is in the offing. Going back to my earlier question about how one might organise to try to limit capital from co-opting oppositional demands in moments of upheaval or crisis, what might such organisation look like at this conjuncture, which presents substantial opportunities as well as hazards?

BT It is important to be clear what this crisis is. To be sure, it first manifested itself in the financial sector, but it is more than a financial crisis. It is a very material crisis of capitalism. The fact that the financial sector and the so-called 'real' economy are not as separate as some seem to think would always have ensured this was the case. Moreover, though, the situation within what is generally considered the 'real' economy (the auto-industry, retail, or international trade for instance) is visibly deepening by the day. The crisis is also an ideological crisis for neoliberalism, from which it may never recover. In his end of year address, British Prime Minister (and former Chancellor of the Exchequer) Gordon Brown declared 2008 'A year in which an old era of unbridled free market dogma was finally ushered out.'

There has been much talk of late of a 'New New Deal' or a 'Green New Deal'. Endless parallels have been drawn between the situation in which President Obama finds himself, and that of Franklyn D. Roosevelt, elected amidst the Great Depression in the 1930s. FDR's New Deal was of course an effort to save capitalism from itself, whilst simultaneously heading off efforts by workers and the Left to bring about more systemic change. Doing so, however, involved granting workers considerable concessions which improved their lot vis-à-vis capital. The welfare state was invested in, a minimum wage introduced, and real wages rose.

Although different in composition to that which preceded it, out of this New Deal Keynesianism again arose a politically strong and demanding working class, to which the neoliberal counter-attack eventually emerged at around the beginning of the 1970s. You are right, of course, that some of the strongest proponents of neoliberal ideology – which argued that social wealth and resources are best allocated by the market, because only there can individuals' pursuit of their self-interest somehow be transformed into social progress – were hypocritical. They very often saw fit to intervene, when it was in their own interest. David Harvey's *Brief History of Neoliberalism* describes this brilliantly. However, neoliberalism did largely involve the stripping back of social provision and the welfare state, combined with extensive privatisation and financialisation. The 'deal' neoliberalism offered was very different to that of Keynesianism, but it was a deal nonetheless. In return for increased precarisation and the stagnation or fall in real wage levels, cheap credit was granted to workers and the poor – enabled in part by low interest rates and a deregulated financial market underwritten by rising house prices. (Increased access to cheap commodities produced in China and elsewhere and made readily available on the world market, of course, also played a role.) As the term 'credit crunch' implies, much of this deal is now null-and-void.

Whatever comes next will not be neoliberalism, or not in the form in which we knew it up until now at least. In itself, this is not necessarily a cause for celebration of course. Indeed, there are few immediate indicators for optimism. Both the neoliberal 'deal' described above, as well as FDR's New Deal, were struck in periods characterised by a far stronger workers' movement and Left than we can claim today. It is the balance of forces and the way in which the struggles between them play out which will determine the future, and at the moment the odds do not look good.

At the same time, however, we could of course be on the precipice of a new cycle of struggles. History suggests that movements do not so much emerge out of poverty and immiseration as such, but more in response to perceived injustices and peoples' expectations not being met. The generation of so-called 'Baby Boomers', whose expectations of entitlement and prosperity were formed during their childhood in the post-war economic boom period of the 1950s, have similarly shaped many of those of the younger generation. As many of the Baby Boomers realise their pensions are perhaps not as full or secure as they had expected, and as the younger generations face increasing insecurity, real wage stagnation and price increases, there is the potential for something to emerge which might contribute towards evening the odds.

Without a doubt, capital will attempt to co-opt oppositional demands. But as yet there are currently very few demands (anti-capitalist or otherwise) being articulated, and more importantly: not much of a movement to articulate them. As such, the issue as to how co-optation can be avoided appears a little premature to say the least.

SL Many of the pieces in this book focus on what happens when movements lose momentum, ossify, or flame out, and how new directions may materialise from the impasse. How true has this been within these movements of the global justice movement? Have you witnessed any promising directions emerging recently?
BT New directions, new movement bodies, always emerge from impasses. Antagonism is built into the capital relation, struggle and conflict is always there and always produced anew. And in the process of struggle, desires emerge and find resonances; new organisational forms and political practices are created. Obviously, this should not lead to complacency. There is no automatism that whatever comes next (or might already be here, unrecognised) will help move things in a 'better' direction.

Towards the end of *Move into the Light?*, we talk about the need to flirt with the death of our own movement. Bodies – understood in the Spinozian sense, set out above – always involve 'internal' movement, and are always defined in part by their

157

relation to other bodies. This is no different for the counter-globalisation movement. As 'particles' within the movement begin to move at different speeds, it changes. And this in turn changes the way it relates to everything which is other; or said differently, changes its capacity to affect others. Likewise, as other bodies to which it relates undergo a transformation, *their* capacity to affect – and indeed to be affected – also changes, often transforming the speed and relation between particles within each of the various bodies relating to one another.

If we think about movements in this way, it makes the idea of preserving a particular movement body seem nonsensical. Its very existence, in other words, is *defined by movement* and relations that are constantly in flux. We're neither able to entirely control the way in which the infinite number of particles within the movement's body relate to one another (in fact, usually we can't even identify them all); let alone the precise nature of the relationship to other bodies. As such, we need to be far more accepting of the idea of letting go of identities than is often the case within the counter-globalisation and other movements.

As to whether or not there are any encouraging instances of the formation of new bodies, or an increase in the movement's ability to effect change, this is something that we will have to wait and see. To be certain, though, there is some cause for optimism. I think the current movement impasse *has* encouraged a renewed openness, including towards closer cooperation with elements previously considered by some to be 'outside' the movement – or at least, outside its more radical area. In the global North, the Block G8 blockades of the Heiligendamm Summit – which involved antifascists, liberation theologists, party youth organisations, autonomous groups, elements of the trade union movement, the anti-war and anti-nuclear movements, and others – was a strong example of this. In the South, the Zapatistas, as ever, have been involved with an interesting process of experimentation through the Other Campaign, where they sought to connect their own, indigenous struggle to that of workers, students and other peasants throughout Mexico and the world. Of course, there were problems with and limits to the Block G8 process; and by all accounts, the Other Campaign has stumbled into plenty of problems of its own. But a readiness to experiment is, in general, an encouraging thing.

MO I will just conclude by reiterating (and echoing part of what Ben has just said): the resonance of *Turbulence* points to a general openness and desire for action, outside of dogmatic, sectarian identities and ideologies. This is definitely a good sign. I also think people and groups have matured and learned from what worked and what didn't over the past 15 (or so) years, and these lessons are very much alive in the collective memories of loads of people that are still very active. The US Social Forum that took place in Atlanta about a month after Heiligendamm was an incredible manifestation of this maturity and capacity to improve and develop institutional and coalitional spaces based on taking recent lessons and critiques of other Forums and of organising very seriously.

I also think that recent crises and conditions the world over – including the rising price of food, the decline of the US economy and US hegemony more generally, the increasingly felt effects of climate change – while incredibly distressing and frightening at one level, also pose the possibility of making the issues and struggles that the global justice movement has raised time and time again more relevant and resonant to a broader public. They can also be an opportunity for developing and bringing the lessons of other ways of living to more and different spaces, even those who never considered themselves part of or affine with movements. I think if there was ever a moment in which our movements and the knowledges and ideas generated by them can gain traction and grow, we are there, but it could also go very, very differently. An old and overused Gramsci quote is very *à propos* – we could definitely use a good dose of "optimism of the will," but always tempered by "pessimism of the intellect."

Sasha Lilley is co-founder and host of Pacifica Radio's Against the Grain and author of *Capital and Its Discontents: Conversations with Radical Thinkers in a Time of Tumult* (PM Press, 2010). Michal Osterweil and Ben Trott are editors of *Turbulence.*

ABOUT PM PRESS

PM Press was founded at the end of 2007 by a small collection of folks with decades of publishing, media, and organizing experience. PM co-founder Ramsey Kanaan started AK Press as a young teenager in Scotland almost 30 years ago and, together with his fellow PM Press co-conspirators, has published and distributed hundreds of books, pamphlets, CDs, and DVDs. Members of PM have founded enduring book fairs, spearheaded victorious tenant organizing campaigns, and worked closely with bookstores, academic conferences, and even rock bands to deliver political and challenging ideas to all walks of life. We're old enough to know what we're doing and young enough to know what's at stake.

We seek to create radical and stimulating fiction and non-fiction books, pamphlets, t-shirts, visual and audio materials to entertain, educate and inspire you. We aim to distribute these through every available channel with every available technology - whether that means you are seeing anarchist classics at our bookfair stalls; reading our latest vegan cookbook at the café; downloading geeky fiction e-books; or digging new music and timely videos from our website.

PM Press is always on the lookout for talented and skilled volunteers, artists, activists and writers to work with. If you have a great idea for a project or can contribute in some way, please get in touch.

PM Press
PO Box 23912
Oakland, CA 94623
www.pmpress.org

Preisz, Isabella
First edition

ISBN: 978-1-945649-38-7

Edited by Rhiannon McGavin and Safia Elhillo
Proofread by Rhiannon McGavin
Cover design by Cassidy Trier
Editorial design by Julianna Sy

Not a Cult
Los Angeles, CA

"all of me is writing to all of you
and I feel the taste of being
and the taste-of-you is as abstract
as the moment"

- Clarice Lispector